JUMBO

the
making
of a
secular
boy

First published in Australia in 2024 by Upswell Publishing Perth, Western Australia

upswellpublishing.com

Upswell operates in the city of Perth, on ancient country of the Whadjuk people of the Noongar nation who remain the spiritual and cultural custodians of this beautiful land. We acknowledge their continuing connection to country and express gratitude to elders past and present for their strength and creativity...Always was, always will be, Aboriginal land.

ISBN: 978-0-6459840-0-2

A catalogue record for this book is available from the National Library of Australia

NATIONAL
LIBRARY
OF AUSTRALIA

Design by Chil3, Fremantle
Set in Polymath by OH no Type Co. 12/14pt

Printed by 1010 Printing International Limited

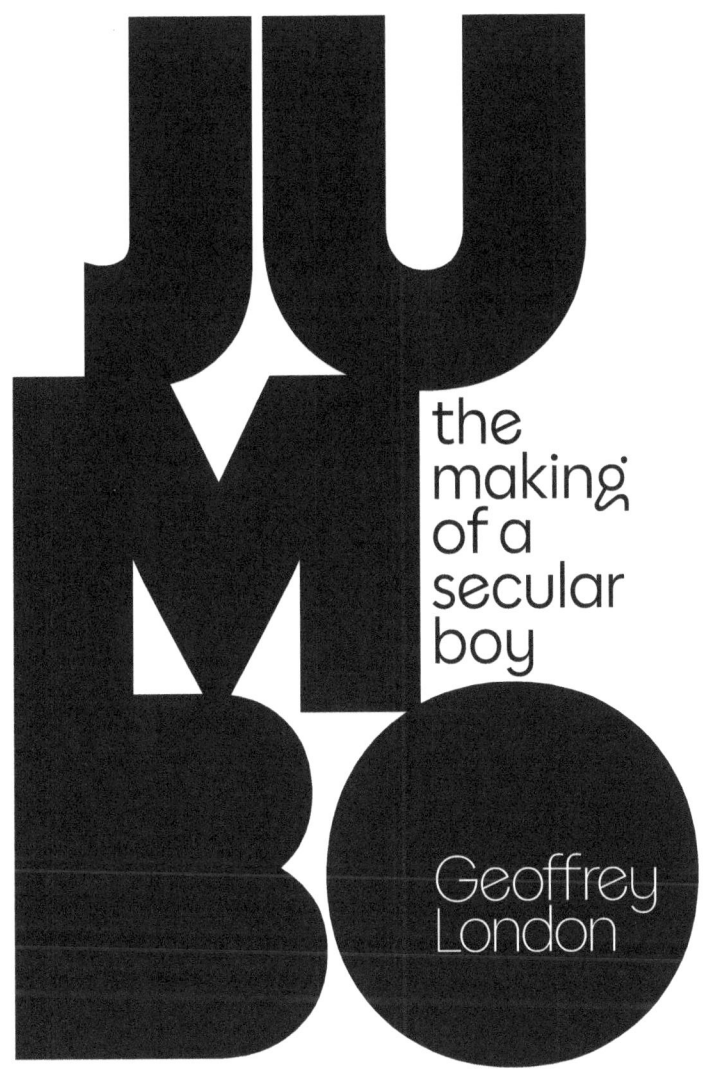

JUMBO

the making of a secular boy

Geoffrey London

UPSWELL

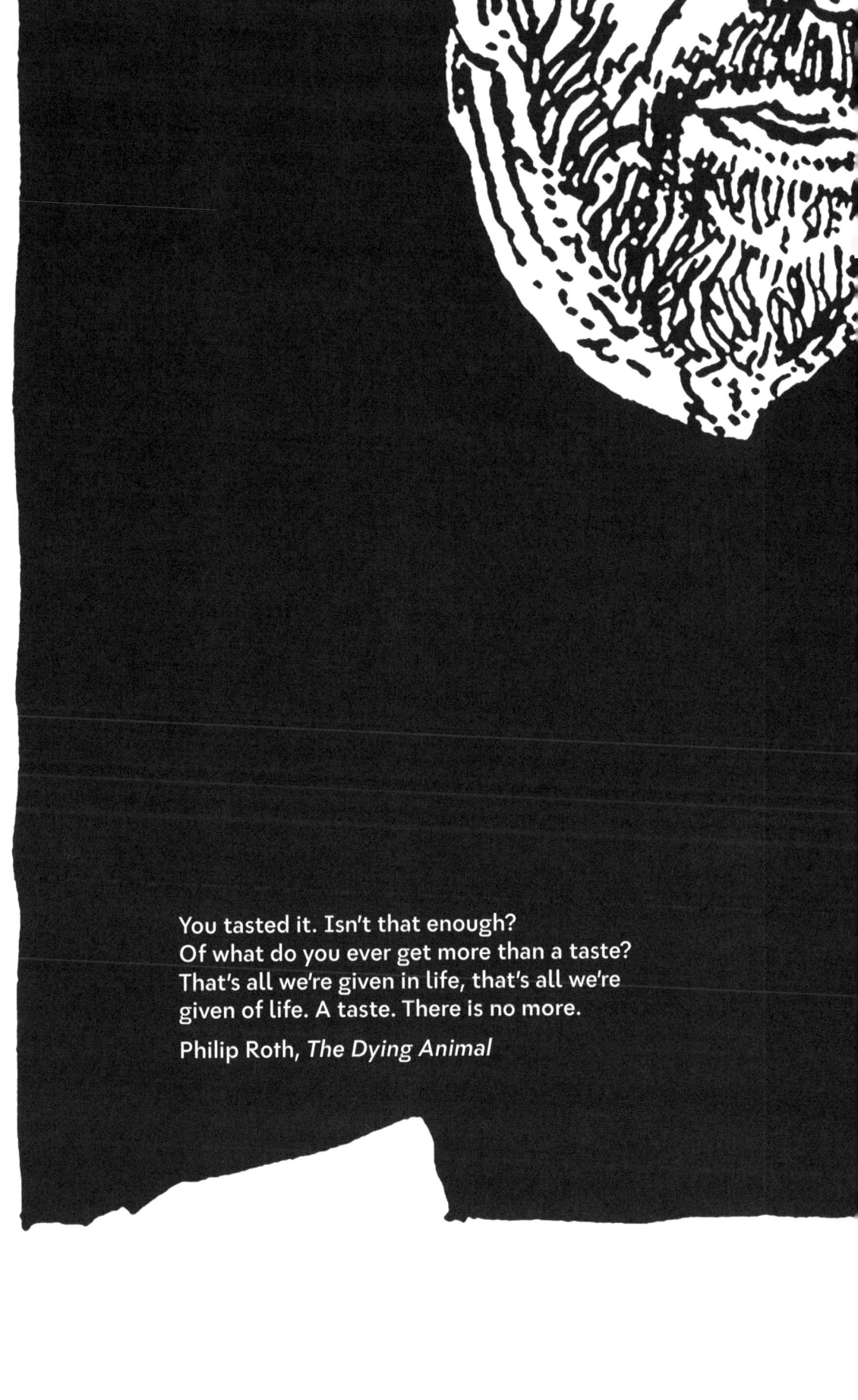

You tasted it. Isn't that enough?
Of what do you ever get more than a taste?
That's all we're given in life, that's all we're
given of life. A taste. There is no more.

Philip Roth, *The Dying Animal*

one

There are moments in a life that seem minor at the time but become major in the remembering – moments that can be recognised as markers, as direction-changers or value-setters in the living of that life.

Choice and chance play equal parts – but also courage and fear, the people we meet, the risks we are willing to take... This story follows formative early moments in a single life trajectory, based on an actual life but with some liberties taken in the telling.

We start with a school photograph taken in the lunch sheds at North Perth Primary School in 1956. The class is in their third year of primary school, what is called Standard 3, and the children are all aged around eight. These faces, already in the distant past, take on a ghostly appearance: what has happened to these young people; how did they navigate through life? What are their stories?

For our tale we could have chosen any of the children in this photograph, but we have chosen the one we know best, the tall dark-haired boy with the hooded eyes, the hesitant smile and a small dark mole between his nose and the outside edge of his mouth.

The life we are following is that of Ray Landau, and our story begins with him as a boy of ten, living with his family in a developing suburb of the most remote city in the world, Perth, Western Australia.

The Landau family in 1958

Ray is the oldest of three children, with a sister between two brothers, and each birth separated from the next by 28 months. The family is Jewish, and they live in a small Jewish community that is contained within the northern suburbs of Perth – North Perth, Mount Lawley and the newer areas of Coolbinia and Dianella, pushing into the native bushland that forms the fragile edges to fast-growing suburbia. This community, a tiny adjunct to the early nineteenth-century Anglo-Celt settlement of what became Western Australia, grew considerably just before and then following World War II.

Ray's parents were both young children when they arrived in Australia in the 1920s. Ray's father, Joe Landau, was born in Jaffa in what was then Palestine, only six months after the violent 1921 May Day riots there that left many Arabs and Jews dead. It seems that the riots began as a clash between Jews, involving Marxists and more moderate Zionists, but the Arabs thought they were being attacked and retaliated. This event, seen by some commentators as the precursor of the post–WWII conflict between Jews and Arabs, the war for Palestine, was a key reason that Ray's father's family decided to leave Palestine.

Jaffa waterfront in 1920

Bubbe and Zayda Landau in Jaffa

Ray's Zayda, his father's father, was born in Jerusalem from a Lithuanian family, and his Bubbe was born in Petah Tikva, an ultra-orthodox settlement from the late nineteenth century that is now part of greater Tel Aviv. Petah Tikva, financially supported by Baron Edmond de Rothschild, was known as the 'Mother of Villages', the first village founded in the 'modern Jewish settlement' of Palestine, and the location of the first of what became many groves of orange trees in Israel.

Ray's father as a small boy, with necktie and his family, after settling in Australia

Zayda was, according to family accounts, an exceptional cabinet-maker, with particular skills in marquetry, the use of patterned inlay veneers in furniture. After World War I, he had travelled alone to Tanganyika to test opportunities for work there. Following a period of time in the city of Arusha, near Mount Kilimanjaro, and for reasons unknown to Ray, he decided to migrate with his wife and children to Australia, arriving in 1924.

Ray's mother, Ethel, was born in the town of Dej in Transylvania, previously a region of Hungary but which, following the Treaty of Trianon after WWI, became part of Romania and, at the time of their departure, unwelcoming to Jews.

Her ethnic background was a mix of Austro-Hungarian, Russian and Palestinian, with a strong family connection to Safed, known as the spiritual centre of Jewish mysticism. Her paternal grandfather was born in Russia in 1839 and, at the age of eighteen, already married and with a child, was conscripted into the Russian Army. With the agreement of his wife he swam across the Volga to escape 25 years of army service. He made his way to Turda in Transylvania where he remarried and adopted his new wife's family surname. Turda was just south of Dej, and the family eventually settled there before moving to Safed in Palestine. Ethel's maternal grandfather lived in Safed and the family tells the story of how, on the day of his eldest daughter's wedding, he went quite mad, to the point where he was locked up in a cave for a week. After this forced isolation he chose to live out the rest of his life atop a small roof, with food passed up to him in a bucket.

Dej during the later days of the Austro-Hungarian Empire

Ethel's mother posing in traditional costume, with jug, in a portrait by Garabed Krikorian

A photographic portrait of Ethel's mother at eighteen was taken by the well-regarded photographer Garabed Krikorian. An Armenian from Anatolia who set up his studio in Jerusalem in the second half of the nineteenth century, Krikorian specialised in portraiture, often posing his subjects in traditional Palestinian costume and performing ages-old activities.

Ethel's parents were living in Safed when typhus became rampant and her father sent his extended family to be looked after by relatives in Dej, joining them after assisting with the epidemic.

The later decision to leave Dej for Australia proved fortuitous as, less than twenty years after, the Nazis set up a ghetto for European Jews in the forest just outside Dej, a wretched holding pen, with nearly 8,000 people transported from there to the Auschwitz concentration camp from where they were never to return.

Later in life, Ray visited the Jewish Museum in Berlin and, on consulting the catalogues containing the names of those who died in the concentration camps, was shocked to see the numbers of those killed who carried his mother's maiden name.

Family in Dej after the typhus epidemic in Safed

The story was told, apocryphal it has proven, that both migrating families, unknown to one another at that time, were headed on ships to Melbourne – but, in both instances, by the time they arrived in Fremantle, the first port of disembarkation in Australia for those arriving after the long voyage from Europe and the Middle East, they had had enough. In fact, with the encouragement of relatives who had earlier migrated to Perth, Ray's Zayda on his mother's side, Mihain, a master silversmith, had travelled there on his own in 1924 to save money, enabling his wife and children to follow. Ethel had been born in Dej in 1923.

Ethel, the small girl in the dark dress, with the extended family after their arrival in Perth

Zayda on the right and his brother-in-law on the left, in their silversmith workshop in Dej

Ray's Nana then arranged for all their household goods and furniture to be packed and sent on, and set off, heroically, for Port Said, where they eventually boarded Commissaire Ramel on its voyage to Fremantle.

While Nana was braving this hellish trip to join him, Zayda travelled from Perth to Kalgoorlie and the Eastern Goldfields where, accompanied by his protective bull terrier, he lived in his car and earned income from his professional skills as a silversmith and jeweller, and his amateur interests, becoming an itinerant performer in operas and theatre. He then established, in partnership with his brother-in-law from Dej, a small bespoke jewellery shop on Pier Street in central Perth.

It was to be more than three years between his and Nana's arrival at the Port of Fremantle.

Ray's mother Ethel as a small girl, having arrived in Australia in 1927 and reunited with her father

Zayda with his prospecting relatives

After Nana's arrival in Perth, the Goldfields continued to hold attractions for Zayda. He spent time there as a prospector and would drive there with Nana to shoot rabbits to help out farmers he had got to know.

The Goldfields was a place with which many Perth people identified during the first decades of the 20th century and, Kalgoorlie, established in 1893, 600 kilometres east of Perth, grew quickly into a bustling metropolis, full of people looking to make their fortunes during the Western Australian gold rushes. It attracted a diverse and ethnically mixed population and their activities were documented by John Joseph Dwyer who set up a photographic studio in the early days of Kalgoorlie. Among numerous Goldfields groups, he photographed the Western Australian Sons of Italy, The Juggling Geraldos, the Yugoslav Orchestra Hrvatski Tamburasi, the Croatian Society, the Rechabites, and the Goldfields Reform League.

The Western Australian Sons of Italy photographed in Kalgoorlie

Guns and rabbits

The Old Perth Shul on Brisbane Street

But back to Ray Landau and his forebears. Both sets of new arrivals lived first in North Perth, just north of the city's railway line, a part of the city that would become the affordable starting place for so many immigrants around the time of World War II, be they Italians, Greeks, Poles, Slavs or Jews. It became the place in Perth where cosmopolitan culinary pleasures could be enjoyed: there was real espresso coffee, gelati in an array of previously unimagined flavours, and food with wondrous names like cevapcici, moussaka, cannelloni, golabki and chow mein.

Reflecting the diversity of its communities, Perth Mosque was built in North Perth in 1906 and the Greek Orthodox Cathedral of Saints Constantine and Helene was constructed there in 1937. And, because North Perth was where the early Jewish community established itself from late in the nineteenth century, it was also the location of the Old Orthodox Synagogue, the Shul, just around the corner from the Mosque, in a relaxed relationship but with a firearms shop on the corner between the two.

Because of ever-growing congregation numbers, the Shul, dating from 1897, with its distinctive Eastern European facade, was extended three times over the years before its demolition in the 1970s. And from 1918 there was a second smaller Shul in North Perth. Located in Palmerston Street, it was known as the Little Shul and it was here that Ethel's father, Ray's Zayda, regularly served as the chazan, the cantor.

Serendipitously and entirely unrelated other than by name, the Canadian composer, Srul Irving Glick, wrote a piece of music in 1979, a quintet for piano and strings, with the title, 'The Old Toronto Klezmer Suite; The Rabbi's Wedding at the Palmerston Street Shul'.

Out the back of the Old Shul was Prince's Hall, a large space used for community events, including public meetings, dances, banquets and Hebrew classes. It was a place to introduce young Jewish people to one another with the hope that they may form lasting unions.

Ray's friend in this photograph taken at Prince's Hall was the daughter of the very good Austrian cake maker and pastry cook who had a shop on Beaufort Street with the family apartment above. The Burgers were good friends with the Landaus and they called in on one another often.

Ray recalls the visits to the Burgers with great affection. The visits were always after shopping hours, and they entered from the car park, through the rear yard, past the bakehouse with its wonderful sweet aromas and, seemingly always at work, numerous cooks wearing white caps and large white aprons. The shop was large and the counter displays that extended around three sides of the shop were stocked with an astonishing array of cakes, yeasted pastries and biscuits. With undiminished fondness, Ray remembers his favourite, the Esterhazy-torte, also the Dobos-torte (both multi-layered), the rich chocolate Sacher-torte, the apfelstrudel, and the shortbread biscuits in a variety of shapes and with a variety of fillings.

Ray and an early friend at a Festival of Purim party in Prince's Hall

The Landaus at a function at Prince's Hall, 1958

Ray also remembers the Burger apartment, with the back door used by the Landaus and a front door from the street with a hall extending to stairs at the back of the shop. Living with a family in a city apartment seemed exciting and urbane, so different from the typical detached house on its own land in a suburb. The apartment had a loggia that directly overlooked Beaufort Street and this provided a wonderful vantage point for discreet people-watching. Birthday parties there were made memorable because the Burgers always hired Uncle Arthur, a kids' party entertainer who knew how to engage children, and who specialised in blowing and twisting tubular balloons into many shapes and figures. His brown Globite suitcase carried all the tricks he needed as a travelling enchanter.

Despite their early appearance together at the Prince's Hall, there was not to be a lasting union between Ray and his young female friend from the Burger family.

The Landaus attended many functions at Prince's Hall and, for the family, it became a home away from home. The Hall and the old Shul were later demolished after large numbers of the community moved to the new northern edge of the city, especially Coolbinia and Dianella, and took advantage of their growing wealth and the post-war way of life made possible in the new suburbs. Because Orthodox Jews should not drive on the sabbath, the new shul had to be within a comfortable walking distance for the relocated community.

A street of modern houses

Among remnant bushland, still with birds, snakes, goannas and small marsupials like bandicoots and possums, new houses were built, with new plumbing, modern kitchens, spaces for cars, and vast stretches of private grass with overflowing sandpits inserted for children's play. New gardens were cultivated with new species of trees that confused the native birdlife. And, every now and again, a strikingly modern design was built, legacies perhaps of the European Modernism left behind by the new arrivals, with butterfly roofs, walls of glass opening onto gardens, bold colours, high pitched ceilings, the most modern appliances and flash new cars parked underneath.

But the dominant model was the American ranch house which, before the introduction of television, was widely publicised in the magazines so pored over as a favoured prelude to house building. These houses became the desired model in the emerging post-war Australian affluence and were lauded as offering all the new modern conveniences that consumerism promised: the breakfast nook, the well-equipped kitchen as the centre of the house, the large hearth around which the family gathered, the broad mantelpiece for displaying family treasures, the hi-fi set, the washing machine, the rooms opening directly to the groomed gardens, and the generous double carport with, in addition to the family car, the table tennis table.

However, the Landau house was traditional, red brick with a pitched terracotta tile roof, and set among a number of more adventurous modern houses. The Landau house had a high limestone base within which the sedate family Ford Zephyr was parked, polished jarrah floors, large rooms, views to a distant horizon, extensive buffalo grass surrounds, a sandpit, a small back shed in the corner, and empty blocks on the left side next door, behind, and over the road.

The Landau house in Coolbinia

Morry and Sue owned the house on the right of the Landaus and Morry collected Phantom comics which he loaned to Ray after he read them. Their house was very modern and crammed with the latest appliances. There was a gate in the side fence between the houses and Ray used to visit and, sometimes, babysit. While still very young, Ray was regarded as mature for his age, reliable and responsible. Sue was Natalie-Wood-glamorous, always strongly scented with a familiar floral perfume, and there was an air of modern excitement about the house, of sophistication, with glitzy cocktail parties attended by smart, good-looking people.

Footpaths were in short supply in the new suburbs and the expectation was that everyone drove from one point to another. Nevertheless, Ray would walk from the house to catch the local bus to the North Perth Primary School, two miles or so distant.

The walk to the bus for school could be rather fraught because of the older schoolkids who would occasionally lie in wait, taunt and often pick a fight. Apart from the fact that they were larger, why they picked on Ray was never made clear, and he assumed it was because he looked a bit different from them and had an odd surname. Ray would sometimes walk with Trevor, also Jewish and a friend from his class. Trevor had a method of dealing with the bullies should they decide to attack. He would turn himself into a whirling dervish with his fists operating like a windmill and doing damage when they landed.

With his shock of curly red hair, Trevor became a frightening Rumpelstiltskin figure, capable of deterring the most persistent of bullies. When he was with Trevor, Ray did not feel quite the outsider he felt when he was on his own, when he was conscious of his differentness from the Christian community.

When he left home for school in summer, Ray would often take off his stiff leather sandals and stash them in his secret hiding place within niches in the limestone walls of the garage under the house. He would then, like many other boys, walk to school barefoot, his toughened soles a badge of honour earned on the hot bitumen surfaces of the roads and the schoolyard.

School was austere and dark inside. There were large numbers of students in old classrooms with high ceilings and stained timber panelling up to the height of the windowsills. The classrooms were crammed with timber desks and their inset inkwells that were filled with fresh ink every morning by the ink monitors, and there was the smell of the linseed oil used on the floorboards. There were kind teachers, clever teachers, bored teachers, ill-tempered teachers...and the students were a real mix – mainly Anglo-Celts, but with a good number of kids whose parents were from different parts of Europe: Italians, Greeks, Poles, Czechs, Slavs and a smattering of Jewish kids from all over. Unlike now, at that time there were very few Africans, Indians, Chinese or other Asians.

The school shed was where kids took their lunch. And lunchtime was an opportunity for getting to know foods from elsewhere. Ray's sandwiches, salami and pickled cucumber on rye bread with caraway seeds, were often exchanged for the dominant Akta-Vite (granulated chocolate with, as described, nutritious supplements) and grated apple sandwiches in white bread which, by lunchtime, was stained brown by the fillings. Yum.

The boys played kick-to-kick at recess and lunchtime, kicking the Aussie Rules football to one another over the asphalt playground. Grazed knees were a common outcome and the resulting scabs and scars were carried with pride. One day Ray watched in horror as a boy running for the ball and oblivious to his own safety sliced open his calf muscle on the sharp edge of a bicycle pedal. The image of that boy being carried away with his tibia exposed became a recurring nightmare for Ray.

The playground was also where the polio shots, the Salk vaccine, were first administered, with kids lining up in long rows to receive their jabs. At that time, there were also the unlucky kids who had caught polio and were left wearing leg callipers over withered legs.

Ray recalled that classes were stopped during the 1956 Melbourne Olympics to allow everyone to listen on the radio to selected events, those that Australians were expected to win. Despite these displays of national pride, 'God Save the Queen' remained the Australian national

Waiting in line for polio shots in schoolyard

Ray's view of Maureen with arm up

anthem, emphasising the nation's deep-seated servitude to its colonists, celebrated two years earlier by a visit to Perth by the recently crowned Queen Elizabeth. As a new schoolboy, Ray joined thousands of other students waving small flags to the Queen as she and the Duke were driven down Kings Park Road.

Ray remembered that, as the result of an awkward incident one day at school, his affections and social conscience were ignited. Another student in his class, Maureen, who sat at the desk in front of Ray's, desperately wanted to go to the toilet and her arm kept shooting up in the air silently beseeching the teacher to allow her to go. But the teacher held firm and would not allow any student to leave the class until the end of the lesson. Poor Maureen reached the point where she could hold on no longer and, amid desperate sobs, she peed where she sat, puddling the floor and splashing Ray's bare feet. As a result, Ray felt real tenderness for Maureen, and outrage at the teacher who had forced this humiliation.

Ray was a good, solid performer at school – but this was part of his natural savviness, not as a result of him working hard at his studies. If he was interested in a subject he would commit time to it, overcoming his natural tendency to laziness.

> *Ray was surprised to discover, later in life, that his parents had coined the phrase 'shitty-shrewd' to describe him while he was still quite young. He was surprised not so much by what he conceded was a fairly accurate reading of him, but by the words used by these clean-speaking folk from whom Ray had never heard a swear word uttered.*

Without great enthusiasm, Ray attended cub meetings once a week after school hours in the school hall, the large central internal space off which the classrooms opened. Cub scouts were the prelude to becoming real boy scouts, with Akela leading the pack, self-evidently wise and endlessly capable, and probably no more than 18 years old. In the school hall, Ray saw on the honour boards his father's name for war service and both his parents' names for winning scholarships to Modern School, the government secondary school for the top academic performers.

Goonderup (an Aboriginal word which, according to the school, meant 'meeting place') Oval was next door to the North Perth Primary School, with Ray's grandmother's house on the other side of it. Nana's house was a treasure trove – she was the migrant who never really settled in to her new country. Ray recalls the large tin shed out the back that was filled with old furniture and tea chests of household goods that were shipped from Dej; the paddock where flowers were grown or, in rotation, horses agisted; the chook pen with its constant supply of eggs; the fruit trees, the grape vines on the side trellis with wonderful black and muscat grapes the like of which Ray has never since tasted, olives, picked green and black, even bananas. Nana had such a green thumb that it seemed possible for her to grow anything. The giant mulberry tree was precious, with selected seating positions – the 'pozzies' – among the branches, and with so many mulberries that they became weapons for those nestled in the pozzies to throw at one another and, later, clean off with green mulberries while squatting in the concrete laundry tubs of the house cellar. Next to the tubs was the large copper, bricked in place and with a small slot underneath for the wood fire to heat the water. The copper was covered with a rudimentary wooden batten lid that looked as if it, too, had been brought from Dej.

Nana was widowed and her children were all grown with children of their own. Her house, originally for the full family, was large for a single person, a generous brick house from the 1920s with a wide front veranda around three sides, and a bay window with a window seat to the lounge room. The western side of the veranda had been filled in to create a small self-contained bedsit flat. Nana had a rotation of Eastern European men staying there, a halfway house between their arrival in Australia and finding more permanent accommodation. These men, Hungarians, Poles, Czechs, came and went at odd times during the day and, even though Ray thought that some looked quite dodgy, Nana knew how to handle them.

Nana and Zayda in their North Perth house

Inside the house there were four bedrooms with high wood and iron beds, strung with wires that sagged, as did the mattresses with their insistent springs. The duck eiderdowns were smothering in their encompassing warmth, and there were stacks of giant down pillows – all shipped from Dej. The lingering smell of camphor seeped from the mothballs spread at the bottom of the rickety wooden wardrobes. The fox stole that hung in the hall, with its flattened face and glass eyes, was always rather haunting. With bedrooms on either side, the long corridor from the hall seemed to slope down to the dining room at its end, with the kitchen to one side and the pantry and bathroom to the other. The dining room table could be extended to seat a large number of people, usually on Jewish festivals.

Ray remembers Nana's hands, with the cracked skin on the ends of her fingers and the short, broken nails from the combination of gardening and chopping and rinsing of food; worker's hands. Nana would allow her grandchildren to swing back and forth the pendulous loose skin under her upper arms. She enjoyed a good belly laugh but, while she was able to be jollied, she seemed embittered, perhaps as a result of her husband dying when she was still quite young.

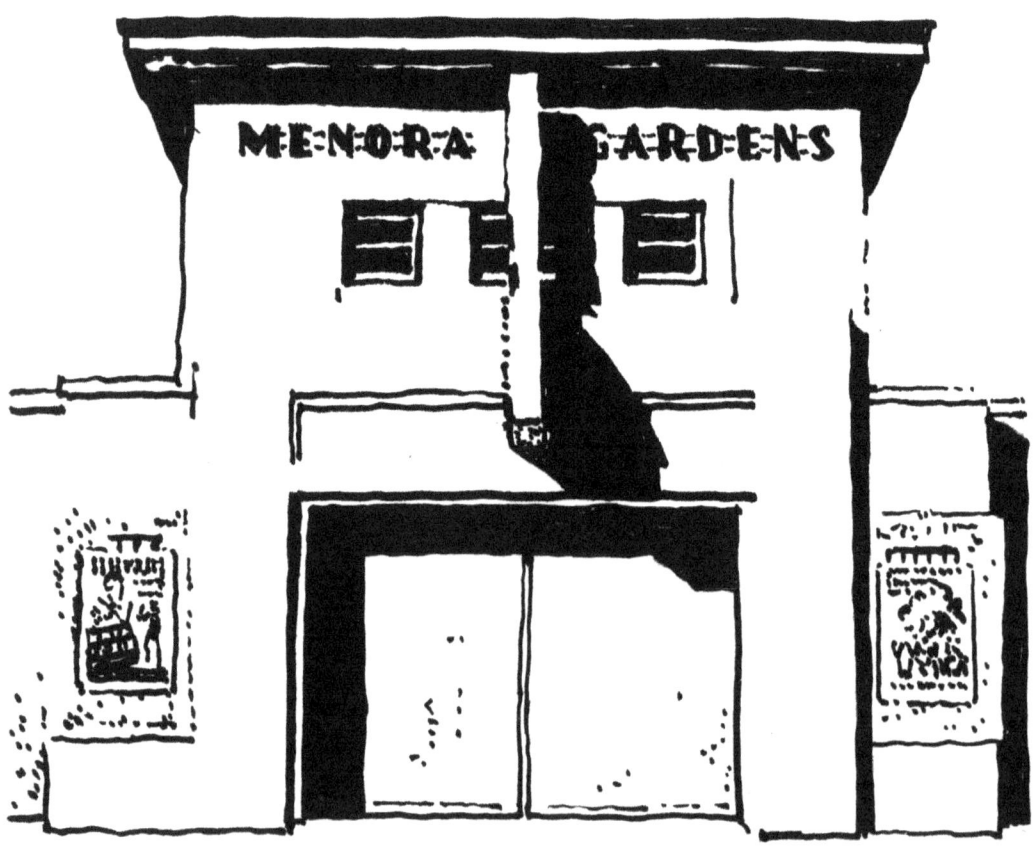

Outdoor cinema

Menora Gardens, the local suburban outdoor picture theatre, was a regular summer evening destination for the Landau family. They watched double film programs and Ray recalls especially the Dean Martin and Jerry Lewis comedies that were shown every two weeks in an extended season (they made seventeen films together between 1949 and 1956).

Ray remembers sitting in the sagging canvas deckchairs on balmy evenings, eating ice-creams, vainly chasing off mosquitos, while laughing at the Martin and Lewis films and enjoying many other zany films with actors like Bob Hope, Bing Crosby and Dorothy Lamour. The fenced-off deckchair section was the more exclusive seating option, with slatted benches available at a lower ticket cost.

The family also went to the drive-in theatres around Perth, the kids rugged up in their woollen dressing gowns and fleecy wool slippers, with the Skyline in Floreat Park being their favourite because it was set in bushland and offered a pre-film ride on a Shetland pony. There was a thrill in driving up to your selected car bay on the bermed tarmac, reaching out to the post between cars and unhooking a heavy speaker, hooking it over the glass in the car window, setting the volume, and settling in to watch a film on the big screen. The quality of the sound was terrible, made worse when many cars would sound their horn at any raciness in the film, but the occasions were memorable and interval treats were always special.

Skyline drive-in

Engagement of Ethel and Joe

Ray's mother, Ethel, worked as the cashier at the nearby kosher butcher, which was also the hub for community gossip, giving her a privileged position of insider knowledge. She always knew what was going on ahead of the pack – who was fighting with whom, whose son was squiring whose daughter, and whose bar mitzvah was coming up. Ray's father, Joe, worked with his younger brother in their father's furniture and cabinet-making factory. Ray can remember the day that his uncle cut off his small finger working one of the saws in the factory – it created quite a stir in the family.

Ethel and Joe were school sweethearts who became engaged while Joe was serving as a forward gunner in the Royal Australian Navy during the war.

This was just as well, because Ethel was having a good time with a particular American serviceman stationed in Perth.

Ethel and her 'Yank' friend

Ethel and a friend 'snapped' walking along St George's Terrace in Perth

The war formed a large part of Joe's later life, with reunions, the camaraderie of war mates, membership of the Returned and Services League (the RSL), and Anzac Day marches. In fact, Ray was named after one of Joe's shipmates who had distinguished himself in a brave act when he rescued a drowning enemy kamikaze pilot. As a result of Joe's involvement, the war also formed a large part of Ray's early life. Ray was very young when he swapped Joe's Leading Seaman cap for an ice-cream, earning Joe's quiet wrath.

Joe had a collection of books that featured the Royal Australian Navy at war and Ray pored over these, together with the war-time photo albums Joe had assembled. There was a haunting photograph of a group of Japanese prisoners of war, captured at sea, staring back at their photographer captor, their eyes filled with hatred. Pasted into the album was the souvenir of a million-dollar bill run up in Hong Kong dollars for a good night out, and then there were the chilling photographs of Hiroshima, just a few weeks after the atomic bombs devastated that city. Joe's ship, the light cruiser HMAS Hobart, was one of ten Australian ships gathered in Tokyo Bay for the Japanese surrender ceremony on 2 September 1945 and he and his fellow shipmates were later taken for a tour of the destruction of Hiroshima. It came as little surprise that, many years later, a large number of the touring sailors were afflicted with cancer, including Joe.

Leading seaman Joe Landau

Ethel and Joe's wedding at the old Shul

A year after the war and Joe's discharge from the Royal Australian Navy, he and Ethel were married in the Brisbane Street Shul. Ray, of course, knew nothing of this event, but many photographs commemorated the happy occasion.

Ray does not recall Joe and Ethel being very religiously active, apart from attending Shul on all the Jewish festivals, keeping a kosher house, and maintaining a social life essentially within the Jewish community. This all seemed part of a lifelong pattern, an unquestioned ritual, expected within the community and a base level of commitment.

Ethel and Joe's wedding at the old Shul

Joe was, however, an active member of the local Freemasons Lodge, where he eventually attained the rank of Right Worshipful Brother. Ray knew about the Lodge because, despite being forbidden from doing so, he had explored his father's thin rectangular brown leather briefcase, which contained paraphernalia necessary for the practice of Freemasonry: he remembers a lambskin Mason's apron with blue trim and tassels, white gloves, name badges, braided regalia and ribbons, and a Masonic diary.

And then there were the annual Lodge Christmas parties put on by the Masons for their kids, with one of their number dressed up in a very grand Father Christmas suit with a full white beard, arriving at the backyard venue on the back of a utility, ho-ho-ho-ing and surrounded by carefully wrapped presents. Father Christmas seemed always to be accompanied by a white-costumed pretty fairy carrying a Christmas star on the end of a long wand.

These parties were distinguished by an endless supply of Peter's vanilla ice-cream, eaten with tiny shaped wooden paddles from small cardboard tubs, and the high quality of the presents, perhaps in compensation for the time the fathers spent at the Lodge, away from their families. There was also ham on offer, prohibited to Jewish people by their dietary laws, a forbidden fruit that Ray enjoyed tucking into. Although it had a Ladies Auxiliary, the Lodge was for

A young Ray at the Lodge Christmas party

men only, and unlike some other organisations of the time it permitted membership by Jewish men. It was much later that Ray learned of the sinister insinuations of the Judeo–Masonic conspiracy theory and The Protocols of the Elders of Zion.

Many years hence, Joe would be disappointed when Ray did not accept his invitation to become a Mason and join the Lodge, although he was very pleased when Ray's younger brother did so.

Joe's parents, Ray's grandparents, lived just up the road in a large house built on a hill with a wide set of steps curving up to the front door. The house was filled with Zayda's furniture creations, impressive artisan items with miraculously inlaid veneers and curved surfaces. The large backyard, the top of a hill, was like a small farmyard, with chickens, pigeons, grapevines, and sheds for making the kosher wine and plucking the birds that had been killed by the shochet. Zayda was given easily to laughter and tears, a sweet and gentle man, but Bubbe was serious, even dour, and was respected for keeping a spotlessly clean and scrupulously observant kosher house.

The extended Landau family sitting on the sweeping set of steps to the front door

Nana and her husband Mihain

Ethel's father, Mihain the silversmith and jeweller, had died while Ray was only small but there were stories about how he would wheel baby Ray in his pram up and down their street, waiting for neighbours to remark on how his grandson looked uncannily just like him. So, Nana was a widow for as long as Ray could remember and she was the grandparent he came to know the best. Her cooking was legendary – the kind of food that made meals very special and memorable. It was a mix of Hungarian and Yiddish, tasty, robust and comforting.

Ray remembers the pastry for Nana's strudel being stretched across the kitchen table with such skill and uniformity that the grain of the timber table could be seen evenly through the paper-thin pastry. And the strudel, particularly the version with walnut and lemon filling, was to die for.

He also remembers the way Nana used the wood stove, with all parts being put to work, even the cast iron tongue that protruded from the two sliding metal doors into the fire box. Nana would lightly spread wood ash scraped from the flames of the fire box onto the hot tongue and then drop on raw chicken livers. They cooked in seconds and were delicious.

Later in life, long after her death, Ray was trying to make a fried pastry (fritlach) that Nana had made so effortlessly and with delicious results. Ray was in a messy tangle and, uncannily, it was as if Nana took control over his hands and twisted and turned the pastry just so, allowing a perfect result.

Joe's sister, Esther, lived with her family just around the corner. She and Sam, a wool buyer who had come from Poland and was astutely assembling a portfolio of investment properties from his earnings, had two sons and Esther was pregnant with a third child. Esther was sunny, generous, always smiling and welcoming. It came as a dreadful shock when she and her baby died in childbirth. At the age of eight, it was Ray's first close encounter with death and the processes associated with the prompt burial and extended mourning in the Jewish religion. Wailing relatives triggered spectral memories from his infancy when Nana's husband had died.

There were other relatives within walking distance of Ray's house, aunts, uncles, cousins, and also many friends of Ray's parents. Some came to Australia pre-war while others had immigrated after the war: Hungarians, Poles, Czechs, German Jews, many with the dark shadow of numbers tattooed on their arms. The Holocaust was so recent and, for Ray, impossible to comprehend: how could humans do this to other humans? Ray's parents had only one book that dealt with the subject. It did so in a matter-of-fact way, filled with incomprehensible statistics and detailed descriptions of locations and train routes. There were very few photographs in the book, small and grainy, but each carried such tragic weight.

Yiddish, the language of the shtetl, was the common language, no matter which country they came from. Ray's grandparents spoke Yiddish as their primary language and his parents spoke Yiddish with them and when they wanted to discuss things they did not want their children to know. Because of his ingrained curiosity and not wanting to be left out, Ray learned a number of key Yiddish words. Yet, because of his desire to fit in, to be a part of the bigger Australian picture, Ray wished his grandparents could speak good English like other grandparents. And he wished that his family did not use odd words like ca-ca and pishee rather than poo and wee. Ray was puzzled why other Jewish boys he knew were happy about being different and with the boundaries set by their religion.

The Australian Women's Weekly was the national carrier of all sorts of important news and information, like what was happening with the royal family or details of the latest set of quintuplets born to some hapless couple. The magazine included homely recipes for sustaining family meals that were often put to use, supplemented by those from the authoritative and weightily titled Country Women's Association Cookery Book and Household Hints. For the Landaus, unless Ethel had the time to prepare favoured delicacies like cabbage rolls (holishkes), cabbage strudel, stuffed chicken (helzel), meat and bean stew (cholent) and baked noodles (lokshen kugel), weeknight meals drew on these sources and comprised meat, usually lamb chops or veal schnitzels, with the occasional beef roast or sausages. The meat was accompanied by vegetables in the form of mashed potatoes and peas or beans, with a salad that was made distinctive by the ingredients all being chopped into small, equal-sized pieces. As a child, Ray always did his best to avoid the salad, but later he could not get enough of it. Sometimes there was fish instead of meat and, incomprehensibly to Ray, Joe regarded the eyes of the fish as a delicacy.

Ray recalls the males at the dining table remaining seated through the meal while his mother served the food onto plates in the kitchen and his sister carried the plates to the table, always, while in transit, picking with her long fingers the choicest tasty bits off the plates for herself. The three

Landau children were allocated rotating clean-up tasks after dinner and Ray became adroit at trading himself out of washing up, a task he avoids to this day.

The Friday night shabbat meal was preceded by the lighting of candles just before sunset and then Kiddush, the blessing over wine, followed by Hamotzi, the blessing over Challah, the distinctive braided bread made with eggs.

Challah

The shabbat meal was always more special than the other meals during the week, often begun with chicken soup and knaidel, matzo balls and lokshen. This was followed by a roast chicken, the best of which were from Zayda's coop, killed by the shochet and which, sometimes, Ray helped to pluck and burn off the obstinate feather quills. The vegetables were roasted, numerous and plentiful, accompanied by eye-watering chrain, a mix of beetroot and horseradish. Desserts, or sweets as they were called in the Landau house, were grand and baked, rather than the usual stewed fruit.

Theirs was a small post-war Jewish community in which shabbat, the festivals and all the religious conventions were unquestioningly celebrated. Ray's favourite celebration was Pesach, or Passover, commemorating the Jews' liberation from slavery in Egypt and the Exodus story in the Old Testament. This event lasted eight days, during which there was a full changeover of the household crockery, cutlery and pots in the cleaned-out kitchen and specific dietary laws observed for the duration. This was a time of unleavened bread known as matzo (Ray particularly liked to eat a sheet of matzo, well buttered and covered in honey), gefilte fish, matzo ball chicken soup, potato latkes, roast chicken and tzimmes. And there were flourless cakes that were a real treat, with the hazelnut meringue the undeniable favourite.

The whole family came together for the Seder night, an extended communal feast set to the script of the Haggadah, which retells the story of Passover. Distant aunts, uncles and cousins all sat with the immediate family around a long table to celebrate the ritual. This included much singing and eating, the drinking of four glasses of wine, the searching for and finding of a hidden piece of matzo called the afikomen, and the posing by the

Seder night

youngest present of the four questions of the Ma Nishtana, beginning with 'Ma nishtana halailah hazeh mikol haleilot?' Why is tonight different from all other nights? The family's Seder night was usually held at Ray's parents' house and the days before the event were filled with the excited hubbub of preparation, as chosen aunts, opinionated and confident women, would be invited to the house to work with Ethel in cooking their individual specialities. Through two linked rooms, the dining table was extended with trestles and tops covered with multiple patterned tablecloths. Ray enjoyed the loud chatter and spirited humour of these days of preparation, together with his self-designated role as official taster of all foods.

If Pesach and the Seder night were joyous and, certainly for Ray, food-focused, Yom Kippur, the Day of Atonement, was the opposite. Regarded as the holiest day of the year, Yom Kippur began at sunset with the grave and solemn refrain of the Kol Nidrei ushering in the day-long fast. The day was spent in the shul, in prayer and focusing on atoning the spiritual self, with no distracting food or water to pass the lips until the dinner that night.

The Maccabean was the Perth Jewish community's newspaper, full of the news of what was happening locally and in Israel. A feature of the paper was the listing of social events and of engagements and marriages. There was the ever-present expectation that Ray and his siblings would marry within the community, that these events would be recorded in The Maccabean, and that they would settle down in that protective community of trusted souls. And the long-serving rabbi would continue to provide them all with kindly spiritual succour.

Ray's father would read every word of The Maccabean when it arrived, with much more ardour and attention than he read the daily newspaper of Perth, The West Australian. And Joe became a contributor to The Maccabean, writing several articles about the sinking of HMAS Sydney off the coast of Western Australia in 1941, a topic about which he carried firm views and the belief that the captain of the Sydney had been made an undeserving scapegoat for the loss of the ship and all 645 hands on board.

Drives in the car

Ray's parents would often take the family on 'Sunday drives', with the three kids in the back of the family car while Joe and Ethel sat, talking and smoking, in the front seat. It was always Joe who drove the car for the family, although Ethel was a very capable driver. These drives could be into the hills, along the beaches, or to visit friends of the parents. Ray never much enjoyed these outings, except when they went to visit Joe's friend and golf partner, Jerry, who was a real jokester. No one could make Joe laugh the way Jerry could, often reducing him to air-gasping convulsions. Jerry had some mystery about him as he had 'married out' and his way of life was different from what Ray was familiar with. Ray was attracted to the 'otherness' from what he knew, of the predictability and seductive comfort of his small community.

Summer holidays included two-week stints at Palm Beach. This was a time of hot sand, sunburn, mosquito bites, calm water and a lot of swimming. Joe was dark-skinned and Ethel was very fair, and, unlike his siblings, Ray inherited Ethel's skin colour together with her attractiveness to mosquitos. The Landau family stayed in an asbestos clad shack with concrete floors and a wide veranda on which they spent most of their time. It was very spartan and smelled of insect repellent and sunburn cream. The shack was serviced by an unreliable supply of electricity and an elevated water tank, which was good for climbing on and showering under after a swim.

The Landaus always holidayed with another family who stayed in a nearby shack, and with whom meals and outings were shared. The other Palm Beach family was also Jewish, but they were Reform Jews, known as 'Liberals', with a considerably more relaxed approach to rituals and practices than the Orthodox Jews. For example, men and women sat together in the shul, rather than separated by floor levels as with the Orthodox. This other family embraced the giving of presents to one another at Christmas time, allowing them to feel more a part of the wider society in which they lived. Ray was very envious of this, as their presents to one another were generous and numerous, and given during the time they shared with the Landaus at Palm Beach.

Chanukah was the Jewish festival that took place around the same time as Christmas and, at the time of the Landaus' Palm Beach holidays, very modest gifts were given, usually in the form of coins. Over the years, as a triumph of assimilation, the gifts given for Chanukah grew to be indistinguishable from Christmas presents.

Palm Beach shacks

When Ray was eight, the family acquired a dog, a mature blue heeler named Tim, to which Ray quickly became attached. After only a short period of time living with the Landaus, Tim was provoked by Brian, a neighbour's annoying child, and retaliated, nipping him on the arm. This, sadly, brought about the end of Tim. On Ray's return from school the following day, Tim was gone, unceremoniously and without the chance of a farewell. Ray's parents attempted to explain that Tim was a farm dog and, because of his attack on Brian, had been given to a farmer. But Ray never quite believed this story and suspected that poor Tim did not have a happy ending.

Tim the Blue Heeler

This was not a good period for Ray and his relationship with his parents. In addition to the calamity of Tim's removal, Ray was subjected to the most determined form of corporal punishment he ever received. The odd smack from a frustrated parent was fairly standard and its effect short-lived, but this was different. The punishment was in response to Ray's own dubious actions and, according to his mother in particular, was a necessary deterrent. Ray had, over a short period of time, stolen coins from his mother's purse. Oddly, he had not used this money to buy anything for himself but had accumulated it until there was sufficient to buy a small ceramic figurine for his mother. When he presented this gift, initial delight gave way to questions about how he had been able to afford it and, quite rightly, none of his attempts to answer were believed. So Ray was formally punished, behind a closed door, laying over his father's knees, and full-strength smacked ten times on his bottom. It was humiliating rather than painful – and Ray vowed never to be caught again.

Ray being punished

Not long after the smacking punishment, Ray had to go to St John of God's Hospital to have his tonsils and adenoids taken out. This was all a bit frightening, but it was also an adventure. Shortly after arriving at the hospital, Ray remembers being wheeled into the operating theatre and a mask being placed over his nose and mouth. He recalls the word 'chloroform' being used, a sweet unfamiliar smell, and being asked to count to ten. Next he knew, he awoke in a vast high-ceilinged hospital ward filled with many beds, all occupied by men, and with nursing nuns in long white robes gliding through the space. His throat felt as if it was on fire and, in his foggy reawakening, he asked for ice-cream to ease the discomfort. His squeaky-voiced request soon turned into a loud and insistent cry – so much so that one of the nuns rushed out and brought back for him an ice-cream in a small cardboard bucket.

Ray needed a pee and the man in the bed next to him told him about the bed pan he should use. Later, he needed a pee at a time when everyone was asleep, and Ray was mortified by the loudness of the sound he made peeing into the empty and reverberant metal container. A fuss was made of him, a young boy in a men's ward, and over the next few days the other patients showed off to Ray, told him stories and jokes, and were sympathetic to his condition, so much less serious than their own. Ray was not prepared, however, when a patient only two beds away from him died. This man had been joking with Ray two days earlier and seemed then to be fine. But suddenly there was a flurry of nurses and doctors and a screen was drawn around the bed. After a while the nurses and doctors slowly emerged and drew the screen closed again. And then a pair of nurses arrived with a gurney and the sheet-draped body was solemnly wheeled away. The ward was silent and, some time later that day, Ray's mother arrived to take him home.

Across the road from Ray's house was a large triangle-shaped bush reserve, sloping away from the high point occupied by the house. It had a small clearing in the centre and this was where the neighbourhood bonfire would be built for Guy Fawkes night on 5 November. This annual event was exciting because it involved burning an effigy of Guy Fawkes, the failed conspirator who had intended to blow up King James I of England back in 1605, and, importantly for Ray, it also involved the setting off of fireworks. There were skyrockets, sparklers, penny bombs, Catherine wheels, throwdowns and more, bought slowly over many weeks from the newsagent and hardware shop, as pocket money allowed, and forming a curated stash to be compared with those of friends. Ray's stash never quite reached the explosive heights of that of his friends.

A Guy Fawkes bonfire

Ray and the local bush did not have a happy early relationship. He found the bush prickly, dry, messy, full of snakes and insects, and unpredictable. The Scaddan pine plantation, however, was only a block and a half away from Ray's house, and this was a treasure of a place to explore. Permanently in shade, with startling interruptions of shards of bright light, it had its own distinctive smells and ground texture, and there were swampy lowlands full of frogs, many black cockatoos with their shrill calls, and mysterious rough-hewn shelters – evidence of occupation by who knows who.

This place was reserved for Ray's own individual adventures and imaginings. He would always go there alone, after school and as the sun was low in the sky. There was the peculiar enjoyment that came from the triumph over fear about the place, of not knowing what you might come across, of the suspicion that crimes were committed in there, bodies and ill-gotten booty buried, covens convened…

Light in the pine forest

Many years later and for his own children, Ray invented a story, The Monster of Menora Creek, based on his time exploring the pine forest. The story was about a young Ray who came across a hidden shelter sporting a smokestack that sent out intoxicating cooking smells. Hidden, Ray watched the shelter and eventually saw a middle-aged man whose facial features and body were disfigured as a result of some unknown catastrophe. This sighting frightened Ray but, instead of fleeing, he remained in his hiding place, anchored by the wonderful smells. He was, of course, spotted by the man, who spoke to him in a kind and gentle voice, inviting him to share some of his freshly cooked biscuits. Aware of the 'stranger danger' and 'Hansel and Gretel' potential of the story, the older Ray tiptoed around this problem in the telling by elaborating the evident gentleness of the man and having them eat biscuits together in a small outside clearing rather than inside the shelter. The biscuits were delicious and thereafter Ray visited regularly for more treats and conversation until, one day, he arrived and the shelter and the man had disappeared from the forest.

This all serves as an extended introduction to our chosen schoolboy, Ray, to what he was exposed to and the base for what follows in his life. Unknown to Ray, his time in this setting was coming to a close. Because of bad business in the family cabinet–making factory and salesroom, Ray's parents will soon pack up their Coolbinia house and relocate 25 kilometres across town to Fremantle, to start a new business and a very different life. And this is where our real story starts.

PART two

Ray's parents bought the lease to what Joe regarded as 'a good solo business', a newsagency in the port town of Fremantle, just around the corner from the local hospital. The family shifted into the cramped quarters behind the shop, a house of sorts with no front door and only a small rear courtyard as the garden. It was an oddly planned house, with no passage, so you had to walk through one room to get to the next. These rooms had windows into a narrow lightwell space that had a glass roof and off which came the bathroom, toilet, laundry and the rear yard. This shop-house was far removed from the example Ray was familiar with, the Burgers' apartment over their shop, oozing classiness in keeping with the quality of the cakes.

Nevertheless, Ray remembers being excited by the change, by the new experiences this shift opened him up to. He felt relieved to be away from all those people he knew so well, his kinfolk, the old uncles who always pinched his cheeks, the gossiping aunts who knew far too much about him, and the cousins who were high-performing students, always touted by their parents and held up as role models for Ray. Ray liked to try different things, and to work really hard at

The mini-village on South Terrace

a single thing seemed to him a recipe for missing out on too much. Perhaps this jack-of-all-trades attitude was his cover for rejecting the application needed for mastery?

The newsagency was part of a small knot of shops, a mini-village on South Terrace, one of the main streets coming out of Fremantle, but still close to the centre. There was the pharmacy on the corner of Howard Street; a hardware store; a barber shop; a 'continental' deli and greengrocer that had just opened, the beginning of what became Galati's, a Fremantle institution; a dress shop; an electrical store; and, in time, a cafe with pinball machines. Behind the shops opposite the newsagency, and down a steep driveway, was a small collection of late nineteenth-century cottages in an almost rural setting of fruit trees, veggie

patches and long grasses. Here, a community of Italian and Spanish families lived a village life with their home-grown produce and flocks of geese, ducks and chickens that would occasionally stray on to South Terrace and cause chaos. Around the corner on Howard Street, and running through to Russell Street, was the leather tannery with its regular foul smells. There was also a timber and hardware yard on the corner of Alma Street and a petrol station on the Wray Avenue corner with a freshly wrecked car out the back and the station owners bearing the still-healing large scars caused by the accident that resulted in the wreck. Ray can remember scouring the wreck with the owners' heavily scarred son, looking for blood. This was all so very different from the suburban street in Coolbinia where there was nothing other than houses and bush.

And the people were different. Ray no longer felt like an outsider in this community – he was among recent migrants, people seeking a better life after the war in Europe. Within this neighbourhood of new Australians, Ray's family members were the less-new Australians. There were Italians, Greeks, Spaniards, Portuguese and Slavs, all living in and around Fremantle. Many worked with the fishing fleet, others were tailors, gelati makers, butchers, grocers, importers, market gardeners, leather tanners, all hard-working people starting life anew. For many, learning English was a real battle and Ray's parents, as the local newsagents, were often asked to fill in and submit government and insurance forms. For this service, freely given, gratitude was expressed with gifts like a freshly caught large fish, a hessian bag of crayfish, or baskets of freshly picked produce. There was the sense of a real community, of people openly helping one another.

An old synagogue was just up the road, though it had enjoyed only a short active life in that role before the Jewish community became established in Perth. The synagogue retained its Star of David, hoisted prominently above the front gable end of the building, and went through various lives, with no evidence of an operating Jewish community in Fremantle by the time the Landaus moved there. Although the North Perth Shul was only a 40-minute drive away, the family no longer attended all the festival services, the previous pattern broken by the demands of opening the newsagency seven days a week. At the same time, Ethel and Joe made new friends who were outside the Jewish community.

There was a Police and Citizens' Club right next door to the old synagogue and Ray went every week, without great enthusiasm, to do circuit training. This was the beginning of Ray's enduring antipathy for training at a gym. His most vivid memory of this venue was watching awestruck, with many other boys, the 1959 grand final of the Victorian Football League projected on a big screen. The city of Melbourne was regarded as the Mecca of Australian Rules football and this exciting game ended in a thumping victory for the Melbourne team as they ran away from Essendon in the last quarter.

Old Fremantle Synagogue

Man shooting mad dog

Ray began as a student at the local school, South Terrace, where he found that what he had been taught at North Perth was ahead of the same class level at his new school. This was fine by Ray; it meant he could coast, take things easy, and get to know his new town.

As he was the only Jewish kid in his year at school, the teachers did not know what to do with Ray when there were classes of religious study, so he was excused from attending. On one such occasion, while Ray sat waiting in the school yard, he was drawn to loud noises in the scrubby empty block next door, separated from the school by a convict-built limestone wall. The ground level of the school was quite a bit higher than the block next door, allowing Ray a good view of what was going on. There, a small group of policemen had formed a half circle around a frantically barking and growling dog that was frothing at the mouth. One of the policemen had a rifle and Ray watched as he raised the rifle and shot the dog, leaving it whimpering in agony before he shot again and killed it. This really shook Ray and he had nightmares about it for a long time after.

Ray as cleaning lady

Related to this incident was the time a young teacher at the school, who had just returned from spending time up in the Kimberley, the north-east of Western Australia, brought back two baby crocodiles. They were very small and, if Ray remembers correctly, were each secured on sheets of card. In this form they were passed around the classroom with very specific instructions. Students were encouraged to look closely at the anatomy of the crocodiles but they were told sternly that their tails were not to be pulled. According to the teacher, this action could kill the babies. Needless to say, some in the class decided to test the teacher's advice and, subsequently, both baby crocodiles died. The teacher was furious and, without any confessions forthcoming, the whole classroom was punished by being kept in after school finished every day for a week.

Another school event recalled by Ray was a costume party fundraiser to which Ray went dressed up as a cleaning lady and, with great fanfare, won the prize for the best girl's costume. This caused endless embarrassment for everyone involved, although Ray saw it as acknowledgement of how successful his costume had been. The prize was a voucher to be spent at a local toy and hobby shop. Ray chose a kit-of-parts crystal set, a simple form of radio receiver that does not need electricity for its operation. Ray was proud of the fact that he understood the electronics sufficiently to make the kit work and he spent many hours late at night, with a primitive earpiece, listening to test-match cricket broadcasts from the Ashes in England while concealed under his bed covers.

Blessing of the Fleet parade

Not long after Ray and his family came to live in Fremantle, they attended their first parade of the Blessing of the Fleet, an annual religious event introduced to Fremantle ten years earlier by the Italian immigrant fishermen who, with Portuguese and Croatians, made up the bulk of the local fishing fleet. It was fishermen from Molfetta who first invoked their patron saint, the Madonna dei Matiri, to offer blessings in order to safeguard the fleet during the year. They were joined later by Sicilians from Capo d'Orlando and their Madonna, with both towns becoming sister cities of Fremantle because of the large numbers of their residents who had migrated down under.

The day of the blessing began early with a series of rapid-fire firecracker explosions, sustained for many minutes, denying the town the chance of a Sunday sleep-in, and causing fear and pain for the local dog population. The parade began after Mass, some hours later, from St Patrick's, the Roman Catholic Basilica in Fremantle, and moved through the streets of the town and on to the fishing boat harbour to allow the individual boats to be blessed. It also gave an opportunity for the immigrants to honour both their heritage and their new home.

Ray was mesmerised by the parade. It introduced another world to him, an example of southern Italy coming to Fremantle – intense and fantastic. And it was an introduction to Catholicism – totally unknown to Ray until then – with its Madonna statues, cassocks and vestments, the thurible and incense, the processional crucifix, and church functionaries wearing colourful sashes heralding their roles. There were children dressed in white, sporting angel wings and carrying white fishing floats strung together in long lines; there was the queen of the parade, a teenager honoured by this role and dressed in long chaste white; there were the two large Madonnas, in one instance carried by men in suits and, in the other, by women in long robes; there were decorated banners from the home towns; and the parade concluded with a walking congregation of hundreds who chanted prayers using their rosary beads. The lengthy parade was punctuated by the oompah of local brass bands; there were children in Portuguese and Italian national costumes; and it was led up front by church dignitaries in full regalia walking with local and state politicians. After the harbour blessings, the parade returned via a different route of streets on its way back to the Basilica. In the evening, there was a fireworks display on The Esplanade next to the fishing boat harbour, the likes of which Ray had not seen before. The fish-and-chip vendors did very well on those nights.

Blessing the boats

Another event the Landau family attended early in their time in the port city was the Fremantle Sailing Club Christmas party, held in the bright yellow clubhouse on the corner of Louisa Street in South Fremantle, over the road from the club's slipway and the fishing boat harbour. Many of the crowd of people who attended were customers of Joe

Fremantle Sailing Club

and Ethel's newsagency and the family was made to feel very welcome. The men clustered merrily around the free-flowing keg of beer while the women set out the plates of food they had each brought for the occasion. Ray remembers this event well because he was so gluttonous and he experienced, for the first time, what it was like to be drunk. The food was bountiful and, for Ray, offered a rich range of the forbidden and exotic. There were prawns, crayfish, mussels and oysters; there were legs of ham, pork roasts, sausages and salami. There was even a lamb on a spit – not kosher, of course, but the family had had to abandon kosher meat in Fremantle because of their distance from the kosher butcher. Ray did not hang back and, out of sight of his partying parents, he ate himself into semi-oblivion. Heightening this state, he accepted the numerous offers of Christmas bonhomie in the form of half-glasses of beer, sometimes tempered by lemonade to become a shandy, from the men around the kegs. Ray spent a sleepless night in tipsy and bloated discomfort. The next day, although he was a sorry sight, he felt that the family was now initiated, truly a part of their new community.

John Todd of South Fremantle eluding West Perth players on Fremantle Oval, 1959

The local Australian Rules football team was South Fremantle and its home ground, Fremantle Oval, was one block away from the newsagency. The Bulldogs, as South Fremantle became known, had enjoyed great on-field success in the mid-1950s and the proud club, dating from 1900, proved to be an instant love affair for Ray. The club rooms and dressing rooms were then open access, with photographs of teams across history, champion players and great footballing moments crammed on the walls between the numerous honour boards carrying famous names. Ray pored over the photos and studied the club's history. He loved being around the serious business of caring for bodies that went into battle, the taping of joints, and the smell of liniment used to rub down the players before and after training. The players were like gods, glowing with fitness, skilled, full of banter, and surprisingly welcoming. The senior players were mature working men, about the same age as Ray's father, exuding confidence in their honed footballing abilities and their trust in one another. They reflected Fremantle's ethnic mix, with the team comprising Italians, Croatians and Anglo-Irish, with a group of brilliant Aboriginal players soon to follow.

Once, during a training session, when Ray was playing kick-to-kick with a school friend behind the goals, they tangled accidentally with a group of South Fremantle players running back in an attempt to mark a long kick. Ray ended up with a set of deep scratches on his left thigh that were made by one of the player's boot sprigs. They took many weeks to heal and fade and were borne as a badge of honour.

Ray joined the South Fremantle under-12 football team. He didn't like training much and he wasn't really a good footballer. He was tall for his age and could bullock his way around the ground, but he had no real ball sense, nor ability to read the play. But he did enjoy the games, often played out in waterlogged exhaustion, and the post-match camaraderie. He also enjoyed the palaver surrounding the team and its organisation – in particular, the ministrations of the earnest parents who assumed the various roles of

South Fremantle Under 12, season 1959

team president, secretary, treasurer, coach, properties man and honorary patrons – there seemed to be more of them than there were players, endlessly ambitious for their charges. Ray's teammates were a mix of precocious ability, pugnacious confidence, brotherly understanding and, like him, try-hard space-takers. The team photo from season 1959 shows the young players, serious and arms crossed in unearned triumphant expressions, flanking the numerous office-bearers of the club, and framed in the well–lit photographer's studio by two free-standing ionic plaster columns and a set of ornamental drapes.

Some of the boys carried surnames of South Fremantle players of the past, some were the children of post-war migrants, while others were sons of long-term locals, including waterside workers, the 'lumpers' of the Fremantle wharves.

The lumpers were the lifeblood of the port town: when they hurt, the town hurt. In addition to being essential for the operation of the harbour, they gave the town its working spirit, its colourful and assertive moods. There was a real sense of solidarity in their community, of people who were hard-wired to help one another.

Ray became friendly with a number of local boys from the school, boisterous adventurers and sons of lumpers. As a pack, they explored the town, including its forbidden parts. They used torches to explore the tunnels that were cut into the limestone hills next to the prison, believing the stories that this was where ammunition was stashed during World War II. Wild fennel found a home in these unkempt backland areas and its attractive scent became for Ray a recognisable part, a signature, of Fremantle. They knew about the local brothel and hung around outside trying to get glimpses of the women who worked there while cheekily taunting the more vulnerable-looking clients, many of whom were sailors from all parts of the world.

There was no security on the harbour, nor on the passenger ships that berthed there, so the boys would sneak onto ships, surreptitiously attaching themselves, one by one, to groups of passengers as they went aboard.

Boarding a ship

They explored the public areas of the ships, helping themselves to tempting snacks placed on the timber-lined saloon bars. They also went fishing in the harbour early some mornings, with Ray learning from his new friends how to bait the hook, use the burley, how to feel the fish biting on the hand line, how to land them and then how to clean the fish. They only ever caught blowfish and scaly mackerel, but the mackerel, if enough were caught, provided a great breakfast when butterflied, dipped in flour, and pan fried in butter.

On hot days the boys went swimming after school at what was called Boronia Bay, invoking the sweet-smelling native plant as an ironic reference to the seaweed stench from the narrow sand beach at the end of Howard Street. To get to the beach, the railway line had to be crossed, another home to wild fennel, and a long wall of limestone boulders climbed. The stone wall housed many rats and the boys took delight in spotting and chasing them.

But more delightful was the occasional appearance of a dolphin as the swimmers splashed around a rock outcrop about 50 yards from the shore. The dolphin was always inquisitive and playful, allowing the boys to stroke its unfamiliar rubbery skin.

From the service yards, the pack of boys ventured into the many pubs of central Fremantle, exploring until they were discovered and thrown out. But one day they pushed their luck too far. Having scaled the wall of the undertaker's parking shed, they were caught gawking at dead bodies in the formaldehyde-laden mortuary. This caused Ray quite a bit of trouble.

His parents were severely admonished by the undertaker for having such an out-of-control son who had no respect for the dead, and also by the policeman who, earlier, had interviewed the boys and given them a lacerating telling-off. It led to Ray being removed from South Terrace School with his parents believing that, together with him not doing any work at that school, he had fallen in with a bad crowd of kids. So Ray was sent to a church-based private school for boys, a fifteen-minute train ride away from Fremantle station which was, in turn, a fifteen-minute walk from his house.

The new school, the College, was very different from what Ray had previously experienced. For a start, he had to wear uniforms. In winter the uniform was a grey woollen suit comprising a jacket and shorts, a College badge on the jacket breast pocket, a badged peaked cap that he was required to doff to teachers and senior students, and a tie and long socks banded with the College colours.
In summer, it was matching field grey short-sleeved shirt and shorts with, again, the long socks and school tie.

The College was full of traditions and conventions that he needed to learn quickly, while always feeling like an outsider. But there was a seriousness of endeavour, teachers who demanded high levels of performance from their classes, and extracurricular activities that engaged Ray. He discovered that he could sing and, as a result, became a member of the junior school choir and took a small part in the College's staging of Benjamin Britten's opera, Noye's Fludde. He was only slightly embarrassed to be cast as the male ferret of the pair led on to the ark with all the other pairs of animals that formed the chorus. The females of the animal pairs came from a

Ray in College winter uniform

nearby girls college, adding a little welcome frisson to the long rehearsals. The committee of mothers did a wonderful job of making painted papier-mache headwear for all the chorus members, each animal carefully crafted into recognisable form. By some miracle of photographic records, we can see Ray on the lower left as a ferret, next to his shy partner ferret, waiting with giraffes, asses, deer, antelopes and tigers for their turn to join the other lucky survivors on the ark.

Ray as ferret on lower left

Regrettably, Ray's voice broke quite early and, as a result, he could not rely on his singing voice to hold notes. This was quickly recognised by the choir mistress, and his time as an active chorister was cut short. However, because he was the tallest boy in the choir and formed the apex of the back row, he was asked to stay on for a time, but to mime instead of sing. As a non-singing member, Ray had mixed pleasure and pain in being a part of the choir that won the interschool choir competition held in the Perth Town Hall.

Ray befriended a classmate by the name of Dennis. He was not like the other College boys who seemed unquestioningly respectful of authority and tradition. Instead, he had a disreputable air to him, often missing school, arguing the point, any point, with teachers, and regularly goading Ray to share a smoke with him in the toilets. Ray felt like an outsider at the school because of his religion, because of where he lived, and because his family was not wealthy. Dennis was an outsider because of attitude and behaviour. One day Dennis did not return to school and Ray later learned from an indiscreet teacher that, as he was the son of a gunrunner who had been arrested overseas, Dennis had been placed in a foster home and sent to a government school.

Ray developed quite a fondness for the Black Forest ham in the rolls he bought from the College canteen at lunchtime and, for many years after, the taste of ham reminded him of the horseshoe rolls covered in poppyseed, generously buttered, with their filling of thinly sliced iceberg lettuce, tomato, onion, beetroot slices, lots of salt and pepper and, of course, the illicit ham.

Ray's name marked him out as different from the other boys at the College, where just about every student had a name descended from the Scottish, English or Irish. His name carried with it the suggestion of somewhere else, northern European, and Jewish – someone looking in from the outside.

In the classroom, Ray was a decent enough academic performer and, although he never quite got on top of it, he was fascinated by the study of Latin and its rational precision. He also enjoyed doing art, taught by a practising artist who recognised and nurtured Ray's ability to draw.

But he remained a bit of a loner, and continued to hang out with others who he recognised were on the fringes of the College society.

When he reached middle school, his home class was on the first floor, next to the stairs. This was the stairwell used by the form masters to mete out punishment to misbehaving boys. The boys would be required to hold on to the stair handrail on the landing and bend over so that their trousers were stretched tight. The cane would then be administered, the number of strokes matching the severity of the misdemeanour. Ray found the whoosh and 'thwacking' sound as the cane struck the boys' bottoms to be an effective deterrent.

Caning

Many of the boys could walk or cycle to their nearby homes in the affluent western suburbs, while others would be picked up by devoted mothers. With a small number of other students from the junior, middle and senior schools, Ray caught the train. Often, the carriages were pulled by steam engines, with their characteristic choof–choof sound and smell. Ray was always disappointed when the engines were diesel. The trains were made up of carriages

A dog box train compartment

of what were called dogboxes, individual compartments that seated people in rows facing one another, the rows as long as the width of the train, with doors out to the station platforms on both ends of the space between the rows. Ray would always go to some trouble to secure a coveted window seat facing the direction the train was moving in and which, even better, was on the side of the train that faced the sea when they went past it.

From this favoured seating position Ray once saw a submarine tied up at Victoria Quay in Fremantle Harbour. After reaching the station, he walked across the rail lines to where the submarine was berthed and struck up a conversation with a sailor who was scrubbing the top of the submarine. He, like the submarine and all its crew, was from the USA, a faraway and glamorous place to Ray, and had that wonderful accent that Ray heard on films. Somehow, Ray convinced this sailor to give him a tour of the submarine, an opportunity which thrilled Ray.

Fremantle submarine base in 1943

It had only been about fifteen years earlier that Fremantle had been a major base, second in size to Pearl Harbor, for US, British and Dutch submarines operating in the Pacific during WWII. Ray learned that the submarines based in Fremantle from 1942 to 1945, numbering more than 170, sank 377 ships while losing ten of their own number.

Ray was given a full guided tour which included going down the conning tower, into the control room and looking through the periscope, meeting the radio operator, going all the way forward, past the officers' quarters, past the torpedo stowage area to the torpedo tubes, then back to the crew's mess, where he was treated to his very first hamburger. The crew was friendly, treating him as an honoured guest. Before escorting him back to the quay, they let him peek inside the crew's quarters at the cramped berths and the heads – the bathrooms. As fascinated as he was by the tour, and as privileged as he felt, Ray was relieved to be in the open and again breathing fresh air. He had begun to feel quite claustrophobic and was convinced that he could never be a submariner.

As a result of the tour, Ray returned home quite late and, when he told the story of what he had just seen, his family found it difficult to believe him, although his father, as an old naval man, was clearly intrigued by Ray's ability to describe some of the technical details of the submarine.

Often using the pretext of having to stay on after school for extracurricular work, Ray spent many afternoons in the first year or two of his time at private school exploring the West End of Fremantle after alighting from the train. The West End was a small area of about fifteen irregularly sized blocks west of Market Street. The streets were narrow and tree-less with characterful buildings set right on the footpath. It was as if the streets had been carved out of the solid mass of building. The buildings were a variety of styles, many with grand facades made possible as a result of the wealth flowing from the gold rush late in the nineteenth century.

Streets and buildings in the Fremantle West End

Because of its adjacency, the West End focused on meeting the needs of the harbour and it housed quite a number of warehouses and shipping offices. Ray visited them to study the beautifully made large-scale models of ships often displayed in their foyers and, on the walls, the maps of the world that showed their shipping routes and the names of the ports their ships visited.

Ray collected all the brochures from the passenger and freight companies, poring over the ships described, the exotic places named, and the alluring offers made, for example: 'scrubbed decks and adventure ahead', from the Orient Line. Viewed from his regular train window, and from his West End research, Ray came to recognise by name the passenger ships as they queued in Gage Roads before being piloted into Fremantle Harbour.

Streets and buildings in the Fremantle West End

An early caricature by Ray

The West End also had a number of printing businesses, with their linotype machines clacking out all varieties of printed product. Ray was fascinated by the printing machines and their devoted operators, who seemed to him so skilled at what they did. But his main target was the paper offcuts that were a by-product of the printing process, the paper guillotined from standard paper sizes to match the needs of what was being printed. Often, this was really lovely paper, smooth, heavy, silken, on which Ray could draw. Drawing was something at which Ray was quite good and he enjoyed producing caricatures of teachers and classmates, some of which were published in school magazines.

In addition to exploring the West End, Ray often returned to the South Fremantle Football Club rooms on his way home. The club and the footballers remained a major distraction for him.

There was a small park just around the corner from the newsagency. It had once been a cemetery during the early period of European settlement and the odd bone was still dug up by enthusiastic dogs who roamed the park in packs. The park sloped up to the south-west, with a magnificent old Moreton Bay fig atop the hill. Under the extended branches of this tree was a small set of playground equipment including a long slide that stretched down the hill. One day, when Ray had just started down the smooth blackened steel of the slide, a large dog angrily bound up to the base of the slide and, as Ray reached the bottom, leapt up and bit him on the chest. He still bears the scar together with a wariness of large dogs.

During this same period, the Landau children were befriended by Mark, the son of the couple who owned and ran the hardware store over the road from the newsagency. Mark was two years older than Ray and, while Ray was innocent of any sexual experience, Mark was not. Mark was already in high school and after school he would visit the Landau house behind the newsagency. His favourite game was to direct construction of a ghost train from chairs and sheets that concluded, inevitably, with him sitting at the end of the journey through the train, in his naked and excited glory. Mark encouraged Ray to sexually experiment with him but, after some initial awkward fumblings, eleven-year-old Ray was not comfortable doing so. However, Mark

The Landau kids, Mark, and marionettes, in Mark's backyard

did have other interests, like puppetry, that Ray eagerly embraced.

To help Ray focus on his schoolwork, he was given his own bedroom in the cramped house, obliging his younger brother and sister to share a small bedroom that was accessed via Ethel and Joe's bedroom. With time, the awkward living quarters were becoming more like a home. Ray had a budgerigar that started out life with the name of Peter but shortly afterwards, with the change of colour to its cere, the waxy skin above the beak, became Peta. Peta was a great consolation to Ray, providing him with companionship and birdly affection. Ray believed that he and Peta could communicate with one another through his close understanding of Peta's warbles and chatters. One day, after Ray returned from school, his young brother was in a state of distress. He had let Peta out of her cage and, catastrophically, she had found her way out of the house. Tears streaming down his face, Ray set off to the surrounding streets, calling for Peta in the hope of locating her. It was not to be. In all likelihood, Peta provided an easy dinner for one of the larger birds of Fremantle.

Ray's parents, perhaps partly as a compensation for the loss of Peta, bought a dog for the household. It was small, as was appropriate for its new home, Pekingese, and given the name of Cherry as in cherry blossom. Ray never warmed to this yappy little dog with its temper tantrums, but his mother doted on it and her lap was taken by the dog whenever she sat. Cherry was known in the family for her uncanny skill at hearing the unwrapping of cellophane around a sweet or a chocolate from ridiculous distances. As a result of this and the misguided generosity of her owners, Cherry's teeth quickly became rotten and her breath disgusting.

Ray received the occasional invitation to houses of College classmates, usually for birthday parties but, every now and again, to test him out as a possible friend. These houses, when compared with Ray's very modest quarters behind the newsagency, were epic in size, in numbers of rooms, in fittings, and in extent and quality of garden. Ray enjoyed the dark-stained timber dado panelling on walls, the high ceilings and their exposed timber beams, the extensive bookshelves, the generous fireplaces, the real paintings on the walls, the patterned tiles or timber parquetry on floors, and the large, soft and comfortable lounge furniture. This was a whole other world for Ray, one that he knew was out of his reach. But he did become deeply attracted to and envious of the electric train sets that he was introduced to and played with in these houses. As a result, he invented his own train set, creating a point of connection with his more financially privileged friends. To ensure that the description of his train set was credible, Ray spent hours in a wonderful hobby shop in Fremantle. This shop carried an impressive range of electric train paraphernalia and, with the guidance of the enthusiastic shop owner, Ray studied it closely to ensure that he fully understood his imagined set and that it was as good as it could be. He settled

Selections from Hornby Dublo

on a set of Hornby Dublo '00' gauge locomotives, tenders, a goods van, a horse box and six coaches, with associated signals, station, engine shed and a workable length of track. Not too extravagant but nonetheless impressive.

When Ray described his imagined set to his classmates, they were indeed impressed, but this created a problem as they were keen to visit and see it in operation. Ray deflected all attempts to make a time for a visit and, after a number of weeks and the requests eventually drying up, he thought he was safe, that he had evaded being exposed as a charlatan, or worse. Ray had not thought that anyone would pay him an unannounced visit – but, to Ray's dismay, this is what happened. Alistair McDonald from Dalkeith owned the best of all the electric train sets Ray had seen. To supplement the train set, Alistair's father had built for him an artificial landscape that took up half a room in their palatial house. The raised landscape had tunnels, bridges, trees and cliffs, and was impeccably detailed. On a Saturday morning while Ray was happily reading a Battle of Britain comic on his bed, while eating a chocolate pilfered from the shop, Ethel called out from the shop that a boy from school named Alistair had come to visit.
Alistair had found Ray's address in the phonebook and, while his parents were in Fremantle visiting friends, had thought this was a good opportunity to catch up with Ray and see his train set.

This was not a good moment for Ray. He tried to bluster his way through the acute embarrassment by explaining that the train set was off being repaired. Alistair was unimpressed by this lame excuse and also by Ray's very humble living quarters. They went off together to buy an ice-cream and visit the fishing boat harbour but trust and credibility were left in tatters.

As the elder son of the local newsagent, Ray took on certain newspaperly responsibilities. Joe, his father and the newsagent, learned from the previous newsagent what was called 'the round'. This was the schedule of home delivery to subscribers of the local newspaper, The West Australian, on every morning but Sunday. It involved getting up at about 4am, taking delivery of the bundled copies of hundreds of newspapers left outside the shop, rolling each paper into a tube capable of being thrown and held by elastic bands until Joe could afford the machine that rolled and then secured the papers with glued brown paper. The rolled papers were then stacked into the family's Austin A40 convertible, filling the car to its gunwales, as Joe liked to describe it, drawing on his old navy days. The wearing of a balaclava on cold mornings was also a throwback to navy days although it made Joe look quite sinister.

Joe had committed to memory which houses were occupied by subscribers and therefore needed a newspaper thrown onto their front porch. But the Sunday round, delivering The Sunday Times, had a different set of subscribers and Joe needed help remembering where to throw. So Ray was called on to assist. He would sit in the back seat, surrounded by a mountain of thick Sunday newspapers, and call out when to throw from a list prepared by Joe. He did this by the shorthand that went like: 'throw one, miss

Joe in a balaclava on a cold morning, ready for his paper round in the Austin A40 Tourer

Ray as paperboy

two, throw one, miss three, throw two…'. Ray gained some pleasure from the exactitude of this process but, on cold and very early Sunday mornings, wrapped in scarf and beanie, he would have much preferred to remain in bed.

Later, Ray was given his own paper round – selling the Daily News, an afternoon newspaper and rather more rakish than its sibling, The West Australian. He had a regular selling spot, outside the corner of the Freemasons' Hotel, where he would stand with his bag of papers slung diagonally across his shoulder and chant the sales cry, a lilting lament – 'Daiiiily News Paaaayperrr, Paayperrr…'. He also took time from his spot at the Freemasons' to visit and sell papers in the bars of the West End. Catering to the needs of the sailors and the lumpers, there were more than ten hotels in the tight area of the West End. Ray knew them all well from his previous antics with the street gang but now, selling the Daily News, with a particularly large section of the paper devoted to football and horse racing, he was a valued visitor to the bars.

The back page of the Daily News was graced by the sly cartoons of Paul Rigby and a witty column written by Kirwan Ward. These two larrikin mates were well-known characters locally, and their bar-room antics were widely spoken about, perhaps apocryphally, as their 'limp-falling', a spontaneous rag-doll drop at the bar, alarmed many.

Another early morning event during which Ray accompanied his father was the annual Anzac Day Dawn

Dawn Service at Fremantle War Memorial

Service. Before they shifted to Fremantle, Ray and Joe would get up at about 4am, dress warmly, have a cup of hot milky tea, and drive off to the Kings Park War Memorial in Perth. There, they would listen attentively to the stirring words of the amplified commemorative service as it echoed through the cold air of the memorial grounds. Ray found it quite thrilling, and the hair on the back of his neck stood up, as the first rays of the sun shot out above the distant Darling Ranges, the flags were ceremonially raised to the masthead, and the solo bugle played the reveille after the minute of silence – and this was accompanied by the sounds of birds greeting the dawn: warblers, parrots, the carolling of magpies and the laughing sounds of kookaburras, the 'bushman's alarm clock'. Ray enjoyed the same sensations when he and Joe shifted from the dawn services at Kings Park to the smaller ones at the Fremantle War Memorial. They were special and moving moments that Ray shared with Joe.

Ray remembers, still with great surprise, the time that a large grey canvas postal sack arrived in the newsagency, unheralded, from the United States of America. Wow – from the USA! This distant country seemed to be the pinnacle of all things that could be wished for. Style, sophistication, wealth, Disneyland, Coca-Cola, the list went on...

The sack was addressed to the three Landau kids and was crammed full of brand-new toys – it was like many years of birthday presents all coming at once. This was booty sent to Ethel by one of her 'Yank', as Joe called Americans (sometimes extending it to the rhyming slang of 'septic tanks'), servicemen friends who had been stationed in Fremantle during the war. On returning to civvy life in the USA after the war, this American started a toy company which grew to become highly successful. The toys in the grey sack were like nothing Ray had seen before. Somehow they were a higher order of toy: there were plastic toys, inflatable toys, mechanical and kit-of-parts toys – and they gave the Landau kids great bragging rights, surviving the hands of many admiring friends, a modest counter to the embarrassment and shame for Ray associated with the phantom electric train set.

The sack of delights arrived around the same time as television began broadcasting in Western Australia. That date was 16 October 1959, with the first channel being TVW 7, a commercial station headlined by a daily episode by the 'boy from Bassendean', the now disgraced Rolf Harris and his drawings of Oliver Polip the Octopus. Ray and his family, together with others from nearby houses,

Early days of TV in Perth

Mouseketeers Jimmie, Annette, Tommy and Doreen

crowded outside the window of the electrical store over the road from the newsagency to watch the first telecasts. Dressed in fleecy cotton pyjamas and protected from the cool evening by their candlewick dressing gowns and wool-lined slippers, the children were entranced by the small flickering black-and-white screens that introduced them to American series like Crusader Rabbit, Leave it to Beaver, Sea Hunt, Father Knows Best, Gunsmoke, Perry Mason and what became their favourite, the Mickey Mouse Club, led by the Mouseketeer who was every eleven-year-old's dream girl, Annette Funicello.

This was the beginning of the relentless pressure children placed on parents to buy a television set for the family home, and it was also the beginning of a more pressured form of consumerism, encouraged by TV commercials.

ABW Channel 2, the Perth TV station offered by the public broadcaster, the Australian Broadcasting Commission, started six months after Channel 7, and its less commercial, more educational focus convinced Joe and Ethel that it was OK to buy a television set. There were, of course, strict rules put in place about viewing times and what could be watched by the children. Being the oldest, Ray was allowed to watch some shows prohibited to his younger siblings. He particularly liked the private-eye show, 77 Sunset Strip, with Kookie, the ceaselessly hair-combing hipster who started off in the series as a car-parking valet at Dino's, the club next door to the detectives' office, but who, in time, ascended to become what he so clearly desired to be, one of the glamorous private eyes.

Sunday night was for watching Disneyland where, according to its founder, all your dreams could come true, and was accompanied, for the Landau family, by bountiful supplies of chopped eggs and onion spread on buttered toast and seasoned with lashings of salt and pepper and a dribble of oil. The TV was in the lounge room, kept warm by a kerosene or oil heater that sent everyone to sleep, and the man-of-the-house was usually the first to drop off, comfortable in his La-Z-Boy recliner-rocker.

Kookie

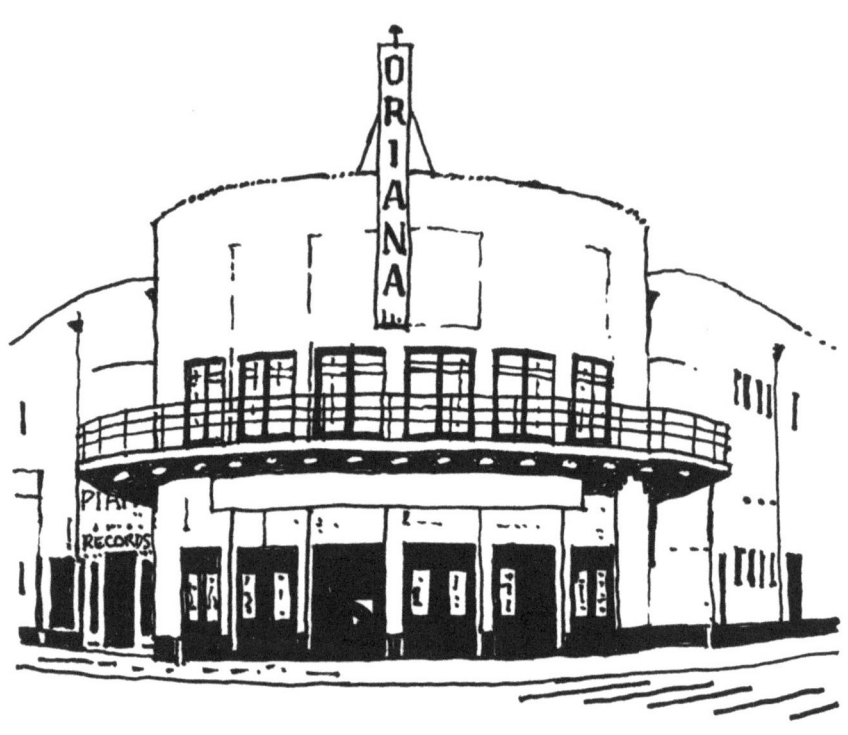

Ray became a regular at the kids-only Saturday matinees at Hoyts Fremantle, later named the Oriana, an art deco cinema on a prominent Fremantle corner not very far from the newsagency. For the ninepence cost of admission, there was always a generous program split by an interval, with either two feature films on show or one film and, before interval, a series of shorter films including the Movietone news and serials like The Phantom or The Lone Ranger.

The full-length features were usually Westerns with the cowboys always triumphing over what were portrayed as the troublesome 'Red Indians'. These afternoons spent in the dark were regularly disturbed by the theatre manager who would patrol the aisles, sweep a torch across the audience, and blow a whistle in response to misdemeanours like having your feet on the seats. Jaffas, small round balls covered in a hard red sugar shell with an orange-flavoured chocolate centre, were the confectionery of choice and often used as missiles by those who sat upstairs in the dress circle.

Ray recalls being taken, as a treat, by his parents to see Pillow Talk, a wholesome romantic comedy from the USA starring Doris Day and Rock Hudson. He watched this film

The Lone Ranger, Tonto and Silver

from the dress circle of the Princess Theatre in Fremantle, while his younger sister and brother were left at home with a babysitter because of the sexy nature of the film that was assumed from the title. Ray was developing an appetite for films.

Another appetite being developed was for the chocolates and other sweeties that were on sale in the newsagency, just a few steps away from Ray's bedroom. At night, to help sustain his homework, erratically undertaken at the best of times and always prey to diversions, he would sneak into the newsagency and take sweet booty back to his desk. He reckoned that this was OK because of all the help he provided in the shop – this help was really quite modest, but it relieved him from feeling like a thief. As time went on, he became ever bolder with the scale of his booty and this showed in the weight he was putting on, transforming from a slim ten-year-old into a quite porky adolescent. Oddly, the rest of his family were also becoming more porky. Unrealised by the others, all the family members were taking advantage of this conveniently located sweet treasure trove.

The Landaus, porky, all... even the dog

To make matters worse, Ray had been seduced by a large-format book produced by a national chocolate-making company. Ray's book was titled The World on Wheels, a history of the motor car, starting with Sir Goldsworthy Gurney's horseless carriage and ending with 'a black and silver rocket car leaving the moon for a Sunday afternoon drive to Saturn'. The book was provided at little cost, and it came with a few grey printed illustrations but without any in colour, only empty frames on the pages where the colour images were to be placed. The illustrations came in three sizes, each related to the size of the chocolate block with which the glossy coloured prints were included.

So, to complete the book, a matter of both curiosity and pride to Ray, he had to buy an awful lot of chocolate.

Of course, he felt duty-bound to eat the chocolate.

The 'chocolate' book

Further tempting Ray, just over the road from his school, on the way to the railway station, was the local bakery. It closed its doors for the day just as school finished and leftover bread was given to any boy who asked for it. Ray really liked the soft buns and the horseshoe rolls and was often seen munching on a small pile in his corner by the window when on the train.

All this excessive and unhealthy eating contributed to the making of Jumbo, the nickname Ray was given by his svelte classmates at school, exacerbating his sense of being an outsider. Perhaps it was just the Australian preference for diminutives of names, but Ray liked to think it was a sign of affection when Jumbo came to be shortened to Jum. His size did work for him when his class was introduced, at physical education sessions, to boxing. Ray surprised himself by being able to beat all who were pitched against him in the ring, even flooring one classmate with a big left hook.

But there was one incident that caused Ray to rethink his rampant greed, if only momentarily. This was the ice-cream-on-the-train incident. To get to school in the morning, Ray walked to the train station from the newsagency, a walk as we have said of about fifteen minutes. This took him down two of the main streets of the town, South Terrace and Market Street, and past various shops opening for the trading day. One shop that Ray often called into was Orlando's, a long narrow cafe with a counter and stools along one side wall and a line of tables along the other wall. Orlando's made their own traditional Italian gelati and Ray thought it was quite delicious. Fixed high on the wall behind the counter, there were large-scale models in gaudy colour of the various ice-cream flavours sitting atop cones. It was not an extensive range of flavours, perhaps six, but Ray had tried them all. A scoop of ice-cream in a cone bought at Orlando's could be eaten in the time Ray took to walk to the train station, a neat outcome.

But, on this particular day, Orlando's had run out of cones and there was not to be a replenishing delivery until the next day. Disappointed but not daunted, Ray asked in what other forms he could buy their ice-cream – were there ice-creams on sticks, in tubs? But, no, the only other way he could buy ice-cream was in the form of a brick. This was, as the name suggests, a brick-shaped and brick-sized serving of ice-cream large enough for a family and enclosed within a folded thin cardboard container. The brick was a seriously large amount of ice-cream – but, having worked up his ice-cream desire and faced with the prospect of doing without, Ray decided to buy one.

Orlando's

If he wasn't able to eat it all, he justified to himself, he would bin what was left. He chose a brick of 'Neapolitan', with its three distinct coloured lines of flavour, chocolate, strawberry and vanilla. He asked Orlando's to provide him with a disposable spoon and to wrap the brick in several sheets of newspaper so that it would not begin to melt before he arrived at the station. Thus armed, and rather pleased with his initiative, he set off to complete the walk to the station.

Ray decided he should sit in a dogbox that had the least chance of other passengers entering while he undertook the herculean task of eating the brick. So he went to the last dogbox in the train and took up his favoured seat by the window. There, he unwrapped the newspaper to expose the brick and carefully peeled back the top of the neatly folded cardboard container. To avoid embarrassment, he left the newspaper in place as a kind of sight screen so that, should anyone else join him in the dogbox, they would not be able to see what he was doing. He ate the ice-cream, slowly at first until he realised that, unless he picked up the pace, he would not finish it before he reached the station where he had to get off for school. His strategy of picking the last dogbox paid off and he was alone for the whole journey of eight stations. Heroically, Ray finished the full brick just as the train pulled into his station. By now, Ray was feeling very full and a bit sick. This feeling increased as he walked, with difficulty, to school. By the time he sat at his desk, his head was spinning and he started to feel as if he could vomit. He quickly excused himself from class and shuffled off to the sick bay to see matron.

Fearing he may have done himself some real harm, he told matron, a kindly middle-aged woman, the full tale of his greed and indulgence. She gave him some warm salt water to drink, ushered him off to the toilet, and encouraged him to try and vomit up his Neapolitan brick. He had no trouble following this advice – and matron then insisted he lie down on the sick bay bed and drink lots of water. After an hour or so, Ray was starting to feel a bit better but, rather than return to class, matron told him he should go home and take it easy for the rest of the day, an instruction he followed willingly.

It was some time, years in fact, before Ray was able to eat ice-cream again – and for even more years, the sight of Neapolitan ice-cream induced in him a feeling of nausea.

Meanwhile, Ray kept buying chocolate bars, yearning for the elusive last pictures he needed to complete his book on cars. In the process, his jumbo-ness flourished, as did his scepticism. He became convinced that there were several pictures that were held back by the chocolate company, encouraging his continuing purchase of chocolate bars in the false hope that the missing pictures may be unearthed.

Ray did enjoy the occasional distraction from eating. As an example, he enrolled in puppetry classes held on Tuesday evenings over several weeks upstairs in the Evan Davies Civic Library, just a few blocks away from the newsagency. The classes focused on the making of papier-mache heads for glove puppets and, for Ray, built on an interest that had been kick-started by Mark from the hardware store over the road. His mother made him the glove parts for several puppets, from the offcuts of materials salvaged from her modest dressmaking on her new electric Singer sewing machine. Ray was able to provide the classes, comprising people much older than him, with a bundle of old newspapers for cutting into strips which were then soaked in the glue paste of flour and water. He started off using an old tennis ball, covered in Vaseline to allow the papier-mache to be easily removed, as the base on which the soaked strips were placed in a criss-cross pattern of many layers and then allowed to dry. Added to the tennis ball shape was a neck to allow the head to be fitted to the glove. Once the papier-mache was dry, Ray used a scalpel to cut the shape in half to allow the tennis ball to be removed and then he carefully glued the two halves together. The head was painted and features like hair, noses and hats were glued on. Once the painting was finished, a clear lacquer was applied and the head came into its own being. As he became confident with the technique, Ray branched out and developed other shapes as bases for the papier-mache heads beyond the sphere of the tennis ball. He used clay and plasticene to sculpt heads with irregular shapes, extended noses and ears and, in the process, his puppet heads won generous praise from the doting older people attending the classes.

Ray holding two of his glove puppets

To operate as a small two-hand puppet theatre, Ray's Zayda gave him the top portion of a wooden grandfather clock that he had started to make but never completed. Apart from being heavy, it suited the task very well, with a large circular opening that enclosed the puppetry action and a roomy interior that allowed the presence of two puppets. Jumbo would prop the clock head between two chests of drawers of equal height and spread a cloth between them to bridge the gap and mask himself, on his knees as the puppeteer. With this portable theatre, his carefully crafted puppets, and a well-directed desk lamp illuminating the action in a darkened room, Ray was able to perform brief bits of puppet theatre of dubious quality for his patient family audience. In fact, he turned out to be more interested in the crafting of the puppets and preparing for rather than enacting their performance, a trait that came to be repeated through his life.

Another distraction for Ray was the new cafe right next door to the newsagency. It was a hang-out place for young Italian men who spoke in their original language arguing, Ray was told, about Italian football, cars, women, and music. The cafe served Italian coffee in its various forms, granitas with brain-exploding potential from the crushed ice, and dolci – it was like a tiny little slice of Italy. It also had pinball machines. Playing these machines became Ray's preferred activity in the cafe – it allowed him to be there unaccompanied while listening to all the conversations – and it taught him where the limits of the games lay before you were deemed to have tilted and the game ended. Ray was one of the few non-Italian customers and became quite skilled at the pinball machines, but never really mastered the table football and its speed, the natural domain of the Italian customers.

Ray on the pinball machine

Living in Fremantle had removed Ray and his family from being actively involved with the Perth Jewish community. As a result, Ethel and Joe decided that some remedial work was necessary and that Ray should attend a school holiday camp arranged for Jewish kids at a site near the town of Pemberton, about a four-hour drive south of Perth. Ray resisted but, in the end, was given no choice. The camp was set in the giant karri forest with one dormitory for girls and one for boys separated by a kitchen and dining room, and recreation hall. Ray recalls spying, with other boys, through the windows of the girls' dorms in search of pubescent naked bodies; swinging from a long rope into a cold dark swimming lake; climbing, with great trepidation, the spikes to the top of the Gloucester Tree, the giant karri fire lookout; and swimming at Fonty's Pool, a picturesque transplanted folly built by Archimedes Fontanini on his farm, the result of damming a stream and forming a large rectangular pool opened for public use in 1925. None of these activities strengthened Ray's later involvement with his Jewish contemporaries. In fact, it helped alienate him.

He found no kindred spirit within the group, not even close, and thought their affiliation with Judaism to be flimsy and unconsidered, a family-led path, well trodden and accepted without question. Here they all were, in the deep south-west forest of Australia, a tiny transplanted colony of Jewish adolescents, none of them children of nature, sticking tenaciously to their learned patterns of behaviour and attitudes to the world. Ray was still too young and raw to make sense of these apprehensions, but he was very sure that he did not want to take part in what he saw as this make-believe world.

It left him confused about where he belonged, and wondering why his parents were so insistent on him remaining attached to this archaic pattern of rituals, this affiliation to a religion that attracted so much baffling contempt and suspicion from so many? Why was it his bad luck to be born Jewish? Why was his life made so much more complicated than it needed to be – especially when he felt so disconnected from the source of the complication? Why couldn't he be like the other kids at school, easily fitting in and with a familiar understood commonality?

Ray thought himself to be an up-to-date boy, progressive even, and keen to partake of what modern-day life offered. He could see lots of impediments to this ambition as a practising member of the ancient, out-of-date religion into which he was born through no choice of his own.

Smack in the middle of all this internal angst for Ray was the serious business of his looming bar mitzvah, the Jewish coming-of-age ceremony for thirteen-year-olds. Feeling remote from the religious festivals and processes and, worse, from any commitment to Judaism, the scary demands involved in learning and then performing the bar mitzvah rituals, together with all the expectations placed on him, alarmed Ray.

And this is the subject of the next part of our tale...

three

We left Ray with the task, reluctant as he was, of becoming prepared for his bar mitzvah, for his ascension to adulthood.

On Sunday mornings, when younger and living in Coolbinia, Ray was taken with other Jewish kids to attend Hebrew School conducted in Prince's Hall, the building that was set in the grounds of the Shul. Here, the kids were taught the Hebrew alphabet, the history of the Jews, and the meaning of the religious festivals. While he did not learn the Hebrew language, he was able to learn how to read and pronounce the alphabet, and this was a necessary tool in his bar mitzvah preparations.

To get himself ready for the bar mitzvah and, he felt, with some resentment, to represent his absent family within the Jewish community, Ray travelled to the Shul in Perth every Saturday for twelve months from the age of twelve. The pattern of the day was repeated each time, with only minor variations. From Fremantle, he caught a designated morning train to Perth and on the way, at Cottesloe station, a distant aunt by the name of Lilly Berenstein would board the train and travel with him. They left the train at Perth station and then walked together for about fifteen minutes to the Shul, where Lilly was a regular attendee.

They both looked very out of place among the relaxed Saturday morning crowds on the train and on the Perth streets: Lilly, in a cloud of sweet perfume, dressed in her best clothes from years before, and carrying a black leather handbag and gloves. She almost always wore a musty fox stole with its squashed head hanging over one shoulder, a hat devoid of flourish but with a strip of voile along the leading edge, thick opaque stockings and low-heeled sensible shoes. Ray wore a grey jacket, a shirt and tie, and trousers that nearly matched the jacket. He carried a blue satin bag, with decorative white stitching, containing his tallis, siddur and yarmulke: the prayer shawl, prayer book and skullcap, all required for the shul service.

Lilly Berenstein

Ray with tallis and siddur

Ray was surprisingly unselfconscious about these accompanied journeys, and what must have seemed the eccentricity of Lilly's and his way of dressing. How was this so, and why was Ray complying with the expectations of him taking on the bar mitzvah rituals? It was all part of an arrangement he had made with his parents in which he had agreed to participate fully in the bar mitzvah process and, in turn, his parents had agreed that following the bar mitzvah, the decision to continue or not as a practising Jew was entirely Ray's choice. This was a hard-won agreement, negotiated with high emotion over many nights in the house behind the newsagency. After his brother and sister had gone to bed, Ethel, Joe and Ray took up their seats around the kitchen table and there were tears and there was righteous passion. Ray had argued that the bar mitzvah meant nothing to him, that he had no belief in a higher power, and that, to him, the rituals of Judaism seemed antiquated and irrelevant to his life. At first, his parents were unflinching in their insistence that their first-born son follow the path laid down by their forebears for many centuries. Ray had tapped into something so primal for Joe and Ethel, so unquestionable that anything deviating from it was to be seen as a failure on their part. But Ray surprised even himself by the conviction of his feelings and arguments.

It was Joe who first showed signs of concession and acceptance of Ray's arguments and that, perhaps, it did not mean they had failed him but that they had raised a boy who could think for himself. Ray eagerly supported this interpretation. Perhaps it was Joe's greater worldliness, a result of his time in the navy, that allowed a broader view of religion. Ethel remained resistant but realised she was heading for defeat and finally, resentfully, yielded. She was cool and distant towards Ray for some time after.

Despite his victory, Ray felt terrible for his parents. He knew it was a form of blackmail that he had used to negotiate, with this outcome, the lesser of two awful possibilities for his parents, saving them the mortification of their son not going through bar mitzvah. And, for them, the hope flickered that Ray may make the choice, having been ennobled by his bar mitzvah and assumption of adulthood, to continue in the faith.

Ray felt he had no choice but to do what he did; he could not have continued to bar mitzvah without such an agreement and a resolution to his growing commitment to secularism – although, at that time, he was not familiar with the term. So he decided that rather than treat the process of his bar mitzvah as a form of painful purgatory, he would take it on as a detached spectator, interested in the ritualised minutiae and setting achievement goals for himself. In making the commitment to be a great bar mitzvah performer, he was going to leave his religion with a bang!

Ray and Lilly always arrived at the Shul about halfway through the Saturday morning service and, while Lilly climbed the stairs to join the other women of the congregation, Ray joined his grandfather and uncle in their dark jarrah pews, paid for and designated by name plates fixed to the back rail. Without desiring to emulate them, Ray was nevertheless quietly respectful of the highly religious men in shul, wrapped in their tallises and davening from the prayers in their siddurs, rocking their bodies and moving their lips as their forebears would have done over hundreds of years. The mystical text Zohar suggests that when a Jew reads from the siddur, or engages with the Torah, their soul sets alight and they rock like a candle flame. Ray was less respectful of those attending shul in order to be seen doing so, who read, concealed within their siddurs, guides to improving their golf swings.

The Shul was not a quiet place during services, at times becoming quite noisy, and the shamas, the shul manager, would often have to give the newel at the top of the stairs to the bimah a few good thwacks in an attempt to restore order and sufficient quiet for the service to be heard.

The rabbi and his beloved wife

The rabbi always offered a 'speech', a sermon in which he would refer to the section of the Torah being read that day, the upcoming religious events, and the role of the Jewry in broader society. He spoke warmly and modestly, with a soft accent that revealed his English origins, and often glanced up to the balcony edge closest to his lectern, where his wife sat. It was a very public love affair.

Ray recalls a period when the regular rabbi was forced to take sick leave and he was replaced by a fire-and-brimstone rabbi from elsewhere. This rabbi was full of bombast about what he claimed as the privileged place of the Jews, the 'chosen people'; he hectored the congregation about the dangers of diluting the blood, of marriages outside the religion. And, in doing so, he used a Yiddish phrase that Ray never forgot: shiksa krikher, his way of referring, with disgust, to those Jewish men who pursued or 'crawled after' non-Jewish women. He allowed Ray to feel more comfortable about the decision he had come to.

Following the shul service, Ray would meet up with one of his grandparents, either his Nana or his Zayda, and be driven, in turn, to one of their houses for lunch. Zayda would drive him to their big house on the hill, where Bubbe remained during the shul service because it was too far for her to walk and she refused to be driven on shabbat. Bubbe's lunches were always lukewarm, having sat in the sealed woodstove from the night before because of the edict that prohibits cooking on shabbat. Nevertheless, her cholent was always welcome, as was her roast pigeon.

Nana, more wilful than Bubbe, allowed herself to be flexible with sabbath laws and enjoyed cooking for her keenly appreciative first grandson. As a result, the range of food was varied, delicious and hot. As a bonus, Nana's pantry was a treasure trove, inviting discoveries and indulgences. The pantry had jar after jar of pickled vegetables, olives, preserves and jams, dried fruits, mixed nuts, fermenting ginger beer, and tins of tasty homemade biscuits and cakes. Ray remembers the delicious quince paste stored in its decorated deep square tin container with its heavy hinged lid. The paste was cut into layers of diamond shapes, dusted with icing sugar, and separated from the next layer by greaseproof paper. The problem Ray faced when he poached the quince paste was leaving clear evidence of his actions if he took only a few pieces. So, to minimise the evidence, he felt compelled, always, to eat the whole top layer.

There was a quirky and earthy aspect to Nana that always fascinated Ray. For example, while she had no understanding of the game of cricket, nor of the benefits of shining one side of the cricket ball to encourage its swing when bowled, she was endlessly fascinated by the sight of grown men brazenly, in front of the television cameras, rubbing the cricket ball up and down in their groin.

After the lunches, at an agreed time, Ray's Uncle Danny, his father's younger brother and the one who had lost his finger in the factory, would come and pick him up in his car. He drove Ray back to the Shul where, in the house next door, he took lessons from the Shul's chazan, the cantor, in singing the section from the Torah that was nominated for his bar mitzvah service. Ray was intrigued by the double role performed by the chazan in the small Jewish community: he was also the shochet, the person who slaughters animals in accordance with Jewish law.

Like Joe, his brother Danny was a stickler for being on time. So Ray always arrived at the house a little earlier than the time agreed for the lesson and, until the chazan's family lunch was finished, was asked to sit at the table on the louvre-enclosed back veranda where the lessons took place. The table was covered in a dark patterned oil cloth, always a little sticky, and the seats were uncomfortably low for the table. The chazan, a kind and bulky man of few words, spoken with a thick Eastern European accent, shuffled out from the family dining table, his surprisingly long and slim fingers still oily from lunch and, patiently, took Ray through his reading. Ray could not help thinking of the many trips he had made some years earlier with his grandfather to the concrete troughs out the back where countless chickens were hung upside down by placing their tied feet over a hook, their long necks then delicately sliced by the shochet and left to bleed to death.

After the lesson, Ray walked briskly back to the Perth railway station, keen to shed his tie and his Jewish identity, cramming his tallis bag and siddur into the pockets of his jacket. Now the rest of the day was his, what he called Ray-time.

By the time he reached Fremantle station he was ready to embrace what that world offered him, something very different from what the earlier part of Saturday had brought Ray: the well-known intimate patterns of behaviour of a small religious community. In the summer months he would go from the station to the adjacent harbour to see what ships he could board and, if there was time, he would go home, get changed and grab his fishing gear to fish for scaly mackerel off Victoria Quay as the sun set. In the winter he arrived in time to go to the last quarter of the football games at Fremantle Oval and, showing his solidarity and kinship with the local supporters, he would barrack very loudly for his team. Going to the football is the subject of another Jumbo episode with food...more of that later.

Despite his parents' quiet hopes, the intense involvement required to prepare for his bar mitzvah did not strengthen Ray's commitment to, nor interest in, his religion. He had earlier tested his religious faith in the existence of an all-seeing and all-powerful God by focusing on a large Moreton Bay fig tree in Fremantle and asking God to demonstrate 'his' presence by causing a branch to drop, safely of course. This was repeated over a period of time, always without success, leaving Ray a developing sceptic.

The bar mitzvah day arrived and, after arranging for a trusted couple to open the newsagency for that Saturday, Ray and his family, all dressed in their bar mitzvah best and squeezed into the Austin A40, drove up from Fremantle to the Shul in Brisbane Street, Perth. Ray was quite nervous that morning but he was able to perform his singing of the selected section of the Torah without fault, following the rabbi's solid silver pointer with the miniature hand and its

Ray during his bar mitzvah service

Ray giving his bar mitzvah speech

pointing finger as it moved across the Hebrew text from right to left on the scroll. Then, in response to questioning prompts from the rabbi, he recited with animated conviction the thirteen principles of Jewish faith and the Ten Commandments, all in English and again without fault. He saw his parents and grandparents, the women sitting in the open balcony upstairs segregated from the men downstairs, radiant with pride and hope.

The formal ceremony in the Synagogue was followed by a large banquet to which all relatives and many of Joe and Ethel's friends, Jewish and goy, were invited. Bathed in the relief of a job well done, Ray gave what he thought was a well-crafted and humorous speech at the banquet, demonstrating his emergence into maturity and responsibility.

The banquet was held at Rosetta Lodge, originally a large house built in 1903 by Gustus and Rosetta Luber, a prominent couple in the local Jewish community. After the Lubers, the house was converted into a maternity hospital, then a guest house and a retirement home, before becoming a reception centre, the location of choice for many bar mitzvah banquets.

Ray's favourite bar mitzvah present

Ray did receive some pretty good presents as part of the bar mitzvah celebrations. His favourite resulted from the request he made to his parents, a portable record player with a turntable and built-in speaker, all in a rather large flip-top box. The player came with three records that Ray played so many times that he knew every word and each musical beat. Frank Sinatra's 'Come Dance with Me!', Ella Fitzgerald and Louis Armstrong's 'Ella and Louis' (his favourite) and 'Nina Simone at Town Hall'. They were great records, a wonderful entree to a variety of contemporary American jazz, and chosen by Ray's Uncle Danny, who set aside his own love of classical music to introduce Ray to something he thought Ray would like.

He also received a rather nice watch that he wore for many years. Its distinctive face had a black inner circle with a gold outer circle containing the numbers 3, 6, 9 and 12, and radiating bars denoting the numbers in-between. From his Uncle Michael came a car coat, in place of the duffel coat Ray thought so hip and had so desperately sought. Ray thought the car coat a poor substitute. Bought unseen from a Singapore retailer's catalogue, the coat was a size too large for Ray and the slippery nylon fabric and its colour was not at all to his liking. In-between these extremes, he valued his new collection of leather wallets and belts, and was surprised to receive three copies of Leon Uris' Exodus.

At some bar mitzvahs a party for thirteen-year-olds followed the reception and Ray recalled attending one such party during which games like spin the bottle were played ad nauseum, a game in which an empty bottle was spun on the floor and the spinner was allowed a kiss with the person of the opposite sex closest to where the bottle ended up pointing. The next spin was made by the person kissed. Ray's view of such games was coloured by the fact that he had never completed a spin that allowed him to kiss someone he actually wanted to kiss. The games were interspersed with strained attempts to dance the twist to the music of Chubby Checker. Ray was pleased that the opportunity for such a party was not offered to him. He was also pleased that, living in Fremantle and out of the small orbit of the Jewish community, he was invited to very few bar mitzvah parties.

Ray wearing a tefillin

As part of the extended rituals associated with the bar mitzvah, Ray was also expected to learn how to put on the tefillin and the prayers linked with that ritual.

The tefillin comprise Hebrew scrolls contained in a pair of black leather boxes and the leather straps that allow the boxes to be tied to the body. Ray recalled being taken, in readiness for the blessing, through the process of binding the straps with the boxes, one on the arm and the other on the top of the forehead. The principle pursued, he was told, was the linking of the head, heart and hand, indicating a singular purpose when praying. While Ray was intrigued by the objects and the detail of the binding ritual, he rejected it as too extreme and archaic for these modern times.

Ray now felt liberated. Liberated from what he saw as the obligations of bar mitzvah that came with being a thirteen-year-old Jewish boy, and liberated in a broader sense as a result of the agreement with his parents, able now to decide himself, without family pressure, whether the path of Judaism was for him. Issues around his ethnic roots and deeply ingrained patterns of belief and behaviour did not cloud his narrow thinking at this stage of his life.

But, back to the football. After completing his bar mitzvah and therefore the need for the weekly Saturday trips to Perth, Ray was able to attend full games at Fremantle Oval rather than just the last quarter, as he had been limited to doing. He relished being one of a crowd, anonymous but the same as the other South Fremantle supporters, all cheering for the same team and the sense of camaraderie that came from the shouts, the cheers, the groans, all in unison. And when the Fremantle Oval was packed with spectators, home and opposition, Ray could not get enough of the atmosphere and excitement.

On cold days at the football he enjoyed rugging up with a big grey woollen overcoat he had been given by Aunty Sadie. She wasn't a real blood aunt, but one of those friends of Ray's parents who were called aunty or uncle to avoid the formality of using Mrs or Mr or the disrespectful familiarity of using only first names. The coat, a little large for Ray, was previously owned by Sadie's late husband but was in tip-top condition. Ray wore a cap and a red-and-white South Fremantle scarf to complete his winter football outfit. He had his favourite viewing position in the ground, slightly elevated, under the projecting branches of a giant Moreton Bay fig tree, next to the north-west forward pocket, and also next to the van that sold hot meat pies. Ray enjoyed going to Fremantle Oval with its old Victorian-era timber-bench grandstand, the crescent of Moreton Bay figs circling the northern half of the ground, the surrounding limestone wall behind which, on the east, was Scotsman's Hill, where games were able to be watched without paying. And looming up behind the full length of the eastern wall was the forbidding external wall of the Fremantle Prison with its austere gatehouse dating from 1855.

Spectators at Fremantle Oval watching a footy game

1961 was a bad year for the South Fremantle Football Club – they finished last on the premiership table, 'wooden spooners' with only five wins, after having recently enjoyed a number of wonderful successful seasons. The team still had good players and Ray had his favourites. One of the reasons he liked standing near the forward pocket was so that he had good sight of John Gerovich, the team's tall and elegant full-forward who played in a long-sleeved jumper, and who regularly took spectacular marks and kicked goals from a long way out with his deadly torpedo punts. Often, it was the brilliant John Todd who delivered the ball to 'Gero' with his raking long drop kicks that seemed to spin forever. Some years earlier, 'Toddy' was playing in his first season, as a seventeen-year-old, when he won the Sandover Medal, the league's fairest and best player award. In his second season, he suffered a crippling knee injury that affected the rest of his career and forced him to wear a knee brace. Toddy adjusted his game to allow him to play with the brace and the limitations it forced, and he remained a wonderful and thrilling player with uncanny ball skills. The whole crowd would gasp in anticipation when he had hold of the football. And then there was Tom Grljusich, a big bustling Croatian who did not play football until he was eighteen. 'Turkey' Tom became a crowd favourite because he did not have the practised, silky skills of many other footballers, but he never gave up, was very strong and, with his huge hands, took tough pack marks.

'Gero' and the 'Mark of the Century'

Ray recalls one particular game, in cold and blustery weather, in which the margin between the two teams was never more than a few points. It was a tough and thrilling game and, at three-quarter time, Ray was hungry and joined the queue to buy a pie. It was a long queue and by the time Ray reached the pie van, the final quarter of the game was about to start. Ray hurriedly bought his minced meat pie, placed in a brown paper bag with its serving of tomato sauce, and moved back to his watching position. The game instantly exploded with a brawl in Ray's forward pocket and, in the excitement, Ray slipped the brown paper bag with its pie into his coat pocket so that he could remonstrate using his two arms, with the intention of eating the pie during a lull. The game continued in this vein and Ray's attention never left the action.

The game ended with a narrow victory for South Fremantle and Ray ran home in the rain, in an elated state, hanging his coat in the hall cupboard and towelling off after getting wet. The next game at Fremantle Oval was played in fine weather and there was no need to wear the overcoat. The fine weather prevailed for five more games and then there was another wet and windy day for the traditional derby against the neighbouring club, East Fremantle. These were always fierce games, played in front of an overflowing crowd, and with many Fremantle families split in their loyalties for the clubs.

Once he'd paid for his ticket and joined the throngs inside Fremantle Oval, Ray jostled towards his normal viewing position. The game started with some typically robust clashes, with tempers flaring around the ground, but also with some very good tight football. Then the rain really set in and everyone at the ground, except those in the grandstand, was drenched. With the rain came the wind and, feeling cold, Ray thrust his hands into the coat pockets. And, what a surprise! In the right-hand pocket Ray discovered the pie that had been saved there all those weeks ago. It was not a pleasant discovery – his fingers poked into a skanky mix of mould and slime. The pie had gone rotten and decayed, covered in mouldy growths and, once his fingers broke the seal of the crust, it released the most awful smells. It seemed to Ray that people started shuffling away from him, with his right hand covered in this vile stuff that had once been a pie. Ray reckoned he had little choice but to leave the game and get rid of this stuff on his hand and, also, the coat. The crowd, in apparent response to the unspeakably awful smell, parted willingly to let him out of the ground. Just before he reached home Ray took off the overcoat and, having decided that it was irredeemable, bundled it tightly and stuffed it into a public rubbish bin. This became for Ray, after many shame-faced retellings, the pie-in-the-pocket story.

There was another incident around a sporting event that Ray recalled with some discomfort, although of a different order from the pie-in-the-pocket. The VII Commonwealth Games were held in Perth in 1962, the same year the American astronaut John Glenn, while orbiting over the city in February, dubbed Perth the 'city of lights' after people were encouraged to leave on lights in their buildings and to shine torches into the dark sky at the time Glenn was due to pass over in his spacecraft. His descriptive words of gratitude brought international attention to the small remote city and great honour was assumed by its citizens. This seemed the beginning of non-stop demonstrations of civic pride that led up to the Commonwealth Games, which kicked off in late November. The purpose-built Perry Lakes Stadium was bursting at the seams for the Opening Ceremony. More than 50,000 people attended, about 45,000 of them in open seating, fully exposed to the 40.5 degrees Celsius heat reported for that day. The Duke of Edinburgh, on behalf of Queen Elizabeth, was to open the Games. Before doing so, there was a parade of the representative youth of Perth, organised in ethnic groups. Ray can't recall how he became involved or what convinced him to agree to do it, but he was one of a small contingent of Maccabean youth, marching with all the other groups and, like the others, wearing a white shirt, white shorts and white sandshoes. The Red Cross was kept busy attending to the many kids who fainted from the heat. Ray reacted differently – during the march past the Duke, the perennial Prime Minister Robert Menzies, and numerous other dignitaries, his nose began to bleed – not in a small trickle, but in what seemed to him a torrent. Ray kept marching, in formation, firmly pinching his nose and jerking his head back in a vain attempt to stem the flow. The blood soon covered his white shirt and, despite his desire to fade into the crowd, to be one of the many, Ray became very noticeable. He was eventually rescued by the Red Cross and a kind soul helped him with his nose and a fresh shirt, not white and far too large, but this allowed him to rejoin the Perth youth, now sitting cross-legged in circles in the extreme heat in the middle of the stadium grass.

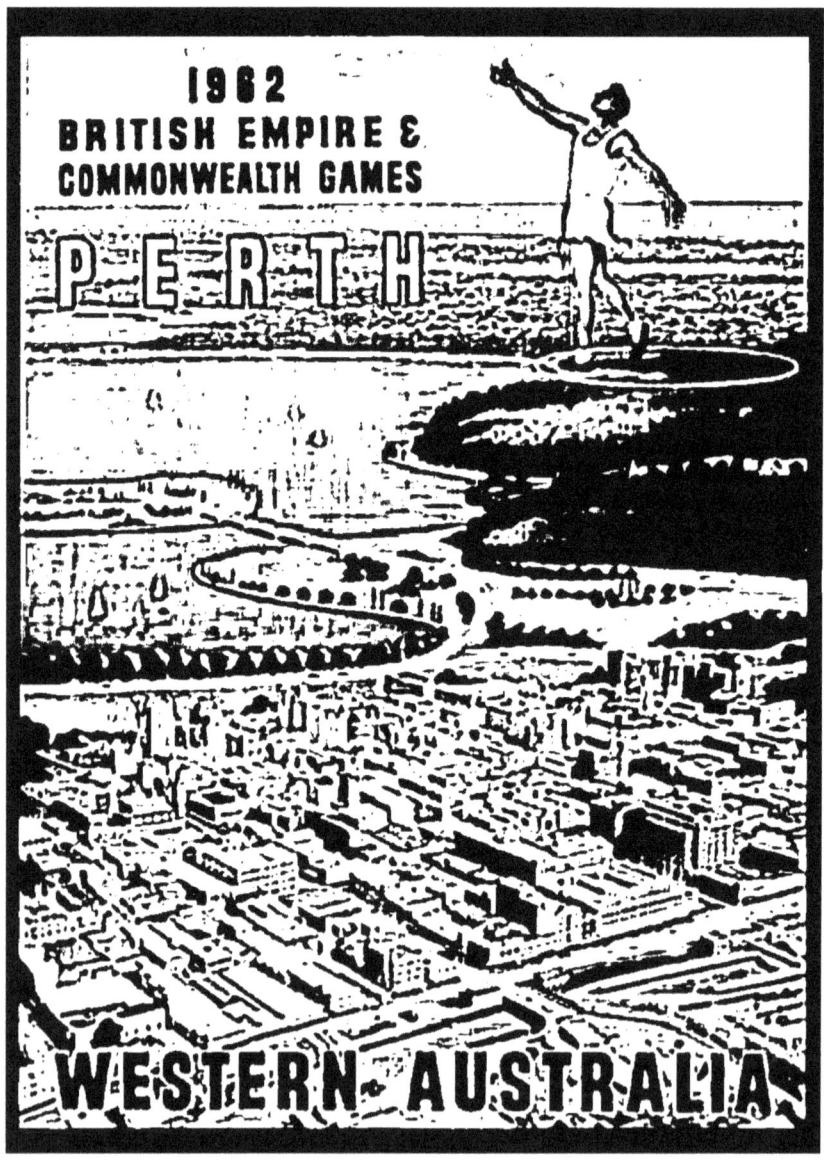

Perth Commonwealth Games poster, 1962

A scene from Through a Glass Darkly

Not long after this event, Ray had a memorable film experience when his Uncle Danny drove twenty miles to Fremantle to pick him up and then drove back to Perth to go to an outdoor screening of Ingmar Bergman's *Through a Glass Darkly*. This newly released film from Sweden was being shown as part of the Festival of Perth program, an annual summer extravaganza of international culture. As a thirteen-year-old, the film was both bewildering and mesmerising. He understood little of its plot mix of family angst, incest and battered psyches, but was powerfully drawn to its darkness, its stark and beautiful imagery and the intensity of its performances. This was an exposure to a whole new world, a world of irresolution, of adults in pain and in doubt. No happy ending was proposed, no sugar coating was offered, but there was a sense of having experienced something real and grave. Ray never knew why Uncle Danny took him that evening to the Dalkeith Picture Gardens, but it changed his view of what film could be.

And, not long after that, there was the first instance of Ray being woken at night by a very pleasant sensation accompanied by an unexpected sticky wetness. While not his usual habit, he made the bed in the morning, carefully covering the wet sheet in the hope that it would dry by the evening. When he went to bed, he was surprised by the fact that the sheets had been changed, without a word spoken by his mother.

Ray and his brother and sister were each given responsibility for one of the three garden beds that surrounded a tiny square of grass in the small courtyard at the rear of the newsagency and its attached house. It was a matter of pride for Ray that the jacaranda tree he planted when they first arrived was now providing flowers and shade. He nurtured that tree, checking its progress on a daily basis, and leaving it was one of Ray's disappointments when he learned that his parents were selling the newsagency in Fremantle and buying one in North Perth. This shift would allow the family to return to an area close to where they had lived in Coolbinia and, importantly for Ray's parents, to bring them back to the Jewish community.

Because of the complexities of operating a newsagency in those years, and the time needed to learn the early morning newspaper rounds, there was an obligation on the seller to have an extended handover period to the buyer. For this two-month period, during which Ray's family shifted out of their house behind the newsagency and the new owners moved in, Ray's parents rented the top floor of a wonderful old house that had seen much better days. It was located on one of the highest sites in Fremantle, opposite the great swollen grass sward of Monument Hill that was topped by the obelisk of the Fremantle War Memorial. The house had a magnificent wide two-storey veranda to the two sides flanking the streets of the corner site. From his viewing positions on the upper veranda, Ray could just see the prisoners exercising at the Fremantle Prison while, of more interest, he could watch the ships queue in Gage Roads and then enter the harbour. He prided himself, after years of harbour-watching, on his ability to be able to recognise the profile of the ships and name just about all of them.

The house on the hill

The house had been neglected and needed care and money spent on it, but was full of character. The body of the house was built in stone with all the doors and windows surrounded by quoins of pointed brickwork. A circular tower on the front corner was finished with a band of terracotta frieze and topped by a conical roof like a dunce's cap. There was a smaller version of this circular tower on the opposite side of the house, going up only one storey. The roof was steeply pitched and several finials remained. The rooms were impressive in size and height and much of the period detail was still intact. The timber veranda had a deep skirt of wooden shingles and infill lattice between several of the upper columns. There were cast-iron brackets at the top of all the columns. It was a very grand house on the grandest site in Fremantle.

The location of the house meant that Ray had a new route for his walk between home and the train station, introducing him to new experiences of Fremantle and to another College student who became his morning walk and train partner. Richard was two years older than Ray and had lived for many years close to the Monument in a gracious turn-of-the-century house. Richard's father had been an officer in the Australian Army and now served the Governor as an aide-de-camp, a term that fascinated Ray and he asked many questions of Richard to understand better what this role entailed. While Ray never quite understood the intricacies of the role, he did understand that Richard's family was embedded in the upper echelons of Perth society, a status for which either birthright or bags of money were prerequisites – preferably both.

Some years later, Ray was dismayed to learn that, only a few years after they had left that wonderful characterful house on the hill, it was demolished and replaced with a row of cream brick two-storey flats.

Because they were leaving Fremantle, Ray was given a choice of schools he could attend. He could either stay at the College, or he could go to Mount Lawley High School, within walking distance of where they were to live. While giving him the choice, his parents were nevertheless keen for him to go to Mount Lawley, where many Jewish kids attended. As a bonus for them, this school did not charge tuition fees, as did the College. But these were not the factors that helped Ray in his decision to go to Mount Lawley. Rather, it was the presence of girls as fellow students and the fact that he could walk or ride a bicycle to school rather than catch a bus and then a train. But first, Ray had to learn how to ride a bike, something he hadn't needed to do in the more urban setting of Fremantle.

So, the Landau family left Fremantle, all with some sadness but with very good memories about their years there. They were now able to see a lot more of Ray's relatives: there was Aunty Jill, whose house was spotless and all furniture and the carpeted floors were covered in heavy-duty clear plastic that squeaked when you sat or walked on it; there was Uncle Leon, who had 'married out' and whose new wife had 'converted'; there was Uncle Jerry, who, as an Australian soldier, had been captured early in World War II and spent three years in a prisoner-of-war camp; Uncle Michael who considered himself, without any apparent evidence to support this assumption, an irresistible ladies'

The Landaus leaving Fremantle – still jumbos

man; Aunty Lois, who never learned how to cook and family meals there were approached with dread; and there was Uncle Danny, a gentle man easily given to tears, with his love of classical music and films. And there was the renewed presence of Judaism, pervasive and persistent. Ray's family unquestioningly embraced it, drawn back into its reassuring familiarity, its known and understood patterns of behaviour. Ray passively withdrew, resistant and stubborn, attempting to forge a new identity for himself, one that was separate from both his family and his tribe.

The Landaus moved in with Ray's grandmother in North Perth, just around the corner from their new newsagency, the house part of which was being upgraded before they could start living there. Ray was very pleased to be able, again, to enjoy Nana's cooking, her pantry of treasures, and to dip into her garden of delights. Nana's house had many rooms and was, comfortably, able to accommodate them all, although a longstanding tension between Nana and Joe was made worse by him having to accept her hospitality.

Nana had a long flat driveway down the side of the house and it was here that Ray taught himself to ride his new bike. His parents had bought him a sharp-looking second-hand bike from Panther, the shop around the corner on Angove Street that refurbished old bikes. Ray quickly learned to control his balance on the bike and, after many rides up and down the driveway, felt sufficiently confident to tackle the ride to his new school.

Ray with Cherry the Pekingese, on his bike in Nana's driveway

Well, Ray almost didn't make it to school on the very first day, surviving a near-death experience. Two blocks from Nana's house, Ray rode down the long slope of Menzies Street to where it joined Fitzgerald Street in a T-junction. While Ray was adept at cycling in straight lines and on the flat, he was totally unpractised at controlling his bike at the bottom of a slope and turning into a busy road. As Ray skimmed down the street he did not apply his brakes sufficiently to allow him time to check the traffic coming on his right and to turn the corner in a measured and safe way. Instead, he burst into the intersection in a wide uncontrolled arc, crossing into the lane on the opposite side of the road before he was able to bring his bike back under control. By some miracle, certainly not Ray's skills, the bike shot crazily between moving cars with some drivers braking hard to avoid hitting him. Ray was normally confident about his physical capabilities but he was shaken and appalled by this close call and rode very carefully the rest of the way to school. He then spent the next week after school, sheepishly and privately, developing his bike-riding competence.

Mount Lawley High School was to provide Ray with such a different set of experiences from those at the College – and this is the subject of our next telling.

PART four

In response to the expanding northern suburbs and the multiplying baby-boomer generation, Mount Lawley High School was established in 1955 and moved into its newly constructed buildings the following year. It was a modern school in every respect, and its buildings were spartan and spacious, arranged around a large central quadrangle with wings of classes heading off in different right-angled directions from the quad. The buildings comprised repetitive modular elements, using aluminium frames, glass, steel, concrete and asbestos cement sheeting. An extensive undercroft offered shade and gathering spots for students, and there were also gymnasia, generous sporting fields, a cafeteria run by the mothers' auxiliary, and the Scaddan pine plantation off to its north, now seriously eroded by expanding housing developments.

Ray found himself placed in the same class as his old friend and protector, the red-headed Trevor. It was a class of high performers and Ray was made to understand by his teachers that he was also expected to perform well. The classes were larger than Ray was used to and made

Mount Lawley High School

so much more interesting by the presence of girls. There were also quite a few students he recognised from Hebrew school days in the past and from the odd bar mitzvah he attended. There were many children of immigrants, with all sorts of names, very different from the uniformity of names at the College. In addition to the Jewish kids there were Greeks, Italians, Czechs, Dutch, Yugoslavs and a few South Asians.

In the classes for 'clever' students, the subject of art was not available for study, not being considered a suitably challenging academic subject for the top intellects. Ray, however, was keen to take art and build on the art-making skills he had developed at the College. So he negotiated with the school to allow him to drop the subject of economics and, in its place, to take art, spread over four separate study periods rather than the block of four linked periods as taken by other students of art. This decision helps explain the totally absent understanding of economics that continues to dog Ray in life. But the study of art provided Ray with the base for his subsequent interests and career. And its stop–start study in four separate periods allowed Ray to establish a more focused and mature relationship with the sympathetic and helpful art teacher.

The newsagency in North Perth proved not to be the vital and bustling local shop that had been the case in

Fremantle. The shop was tucked away around the corner and over a busy road from the local main street, and there was no nearby hospital that, in Fremantle, had provided such a reliable source of sales. Joe did his paper rounds every day and, even though they were smaller than he was used to in Fremantle, he began to find the early morning regime taxing.

Ray contributed to the shop by collecting money owed monthly for delivery subscriptions of newspapers and magazines. Subscribers were split into four precinct areas, and each week on Saturday morning he walked from house to house within one area of collection. Ray approached this task with both trepidation and fascination. Through the common means of the front door, the process of collecting money owed gave Ray fleeting access to such different lives, different from one another and from his own. There was the man who always answered the door while strapping on his prosthetic leg; there was the sweet old lady who always invited Ray in for a cup of tea and Devonshire biscuits; there was the man who kept carpet snakes; there were the many lonely people who just wanted to chat; there were those who claimed never to have the money to pay; and there were the recent migrants who did not yet have English-language skills and whose houses suggested an exotic otherness. There were the smells: of unfamiliar meals being cooked; of pet animals that needed a clean; of people who needed a clean; of alcohol and cigarettes. There was the threat of dogs that barked aggressively from behind the door after Ray knocked, and of pets escaping when the door was opened.

Ray was always relieved when he returned safely to the newsagency after these rounds, removing his heavy leather satchel that contained the receipt book and the collected money that was then counted to reconcile what was owed and received. He felt he really earned the modest payment he received from completing this task. He was also aware of how this experience challenged him, but also expanded his own experience and view of life. While reasonably mature for his age, Ray was nevertheless subject to insecurities and fears, and often felt that he was faking his way through life. These experiences were very real and helped ground him.

Ray's values and personality were forming and emerging in a hesitant and, at times, contradictory way. What can be observed and what could be said of him? He was a fifteen-year-old loner, often by choice, but not always. Even though he wanted to fit in, to be the same as others, he had difficulties identifying with groups. This was a key difference he felt with other Jewish boys he knew who were happy being part of their religious community and with the boundaries it set, real and imagined. At that time in his life, Ray resented something that marked him out as different, that prevented him merging into broader society. He felt, as an individual Jew, subject to all sorts of assumptions and, as a group, unfairly judged. He was a natural sceptic and, as a default, exercised uncertainty over certainty. He harboured lashings of self-doubt and was suspicious of others who lacked it. He learned early the benefits of holding his tongue and keeping shtum, of waiting to see the lie of the land before leaping in. He preferred modesty over ostentation and grand flourishes. He distrusted any praise he received and resented goody-two-shoes who he felt showed him up as being self-interested and lazy. Ray was keen-eyed, missing little, and felt more temperamentally aligned with his mother's side of the family than his father's: indoors rather than outdoors people. A number of these traits proved tenacious and stuck with him as he experienced life and grew older.

Ray became friends at school with Wally, the son of a couple who managed a farm in the West Australian wheatbelt. During school terms, Wally stayed with his grandmother in a large rambling old house in North Perth and he and Ray began cycling together to and from school. They played backyard cricket and fantasised that their poor skills would one day transform to allow them to become test cricket teammates. Wally was a high-performing student with an extraordinary ability in mathematics. Ray was reasonably adept in maths but Wally's comprehension was at genius level. He also had a great sense of humour and a broad smile that rarely left his face. His smile, freckles and open face reminded Ray of that quintessentially larrikin Australian child, Smiley, from the book and film of the same name.

Wally invited Ray to his parents' farm outside Narembeen for one of the two-week holidays between school terms and Ray eagerly accepted. He knew nothing about farm life and nothing about Wally's parents. Ray remembers a long drive with Wally's cheerful father deep into the flat featureless wheatbelt, to a simple rectangular brick house with wide verandas. There were nights made remarkable by the clear star-filled skies and the sharp cold temperatures, eased by the homely comfort of the large wood stove. He remembers eating mutton in various forms every night and his shock one day in seeing Wally's father casually bend back the neck of a badly fly-blown sheep and cut its throat. He had dreams that night of Wally's father with his nearly severed head bouncing around on the stump of his neck as he walked.

He and Wally were introduced by Wally's parents to bridge, a complex but alluring card game. They played many rounds while sitting close to the wood stove, eating freshly baked cake or scones, and chatting happily. Ray was relieved that religion formed no part of these evening chats. During the day they helped with farm chores: chopping wood, feeding stock, repairing fences, and checking on lambing ewes. One day they drove to a property outside the nearby town of Bruce Rock to visit some relatives of Wally's mother. This family lived in a large but run-down farmhouse and, according to Wally, were very wealthy, while all appearances belied that description. Inside the house was an Aladdin's cave of treasures and contrasts. This was a family obsessed with buying but rarely unpackaging what they bought. There were boxes of household goods, with several brands of the same item: vacuum cleaners, clothes pressers, washing machines, kitchen appliances, furniture and even television sets, although there was not yet any decent reception in those parts. Each room in the house was packed with unopened boxes, and the kitchen was filled with leftover food scraps on the table and dirty dishes cramming the sink, while flies buzzed around feasting. The family was also physically unconventional, with the members suffering from what was described to Ray as 'acromegaly', a condition that results in very large hands, feet and facial features.

At the end of their stay on the farm, Wally's father drove the family and Ray to an airstrip about 150 kilometres away in Cunderdin where he was considering taking a job as the airstrip mechanic and leaving the tough farming life. On the way, on a back road, they hit a cow that had escaped from its paddock. Ray and Wally were sitting on the front bench seat of the car with Wally's father driving and the cow dashed out, hit the front of the car, slid diagonally across the car bonnet and whacked the passenger side windscreen pillar. By some miracle, the animal did not break the windscreen. It did more damage to itself than it did to the car. The cow was unable to stand and Wally's father drove off to find the farmer. The car had a badly bent bumper and dented bonnet but, otherwise, was fine to drive. Ray recalled the collision in slow motion, seeing the shocked expression in the cow's huge eyes, and expecting to find himself under the cow as it moved towards him. The lack of seatbelts left all three on the front seat with nasty bruises and cuts.

On reaching Cunderdin the family and Ray were invited to stay the night in the spartan men's quarters next to the airstrip, with its clean rooms and fresh towels but minimal heating. After a very cold night they woke to the sound of a helicopter landing and Wally and Ray rushed outside to check it out. They were invited, together with Wally's father, to come up for a spin over the countryside. This was an unexpected thrill for Ray, who still had not been in an aeroplane let alone a helicopter. Later that day, they drove back to Perth and Ray's rural adventure was over.

Towards the end of the 1963 school year, there came a newsflash on the radio that US President John F. Kennedy, elected only three years earlier, had been assassinated while on a motorcade in Dallas. Ray was shaken by this news and it seemed to cast a pall over the whole world as the details of the killing and its aftermath, the swearing-in of Lyndon Johnson as the replacement president, the arrest of Lee Harvey Oswald, and his public murder by Jack Ruby, dominated the news for many days. Television stations showed graphic footage of the shooting and its effect on Jackie Kennedy, who had been sitting right next to the President, the secret service agents supposedly providing protection, and the watching crowd. Conspiracy theories were immediately put forward and, despite many government and other reports, the full details of the assassination remained elusive. Ray followed the unfolding story with fascinated horror, and terms like 'grassy knoll', 'sniper's nest' and 'running board' took on new meanings as they entered the public lexicon. It was one of those 'where were you when...' moments, to be joined by others, like John Lennon's death, the shark attack death of Ken Crew at North Cottesloe, and the destruction of the twin towers in New York, as the years peeled by for Ray.

Joe would have a 'where were you when...' moment when, on 11 February 1964, the Australian aircraft carrier HMAS Melbourne collided with the destroyer HMAS Voyager, cutting it in half and killing 82 of the Voyager's officers and crew. As an old navy man this tragedy deeply upset Joe and he developed all sorts of theories about its cause. Ray was the sounding board for these theories during a time when the whole of Australia was mourning the disaster.

The damaged prow of HMAS Melbourne after the collision with HMAS Voyager

After a couple of years of struggle, Joe and Ethel sold up the North Perth shop and bought a newsagency/gift shop in the city, with no paper round to disrupt Joe's mornings. This was all done very quietly and came as a surprise to the kids. This sale resulted in the family shifting to a house in Coolbinia, only a couple of blocks away from their old house that they had left six years ago. The new house was in a hollow rather than atop a hill and smaller than their previous Coolbinia house, but it did have a pleasant garden and was quite cosy inside. Ray's bedroom was previously a corner veranda that had been converted to a sleepout, lined with louvres that rattled in the wind and provided close encounters with whatever came out of the nearby open bedroom window of his neighbours, an argumentative and sexually noisy pair.

With this shift, Ray and Wally lived in nearly opposite directions from the school, so they rarely saw one another outside their time together in school. Ray would now sometimes walk home with Trevor, whose house was halfway between the school and his own house. Trevor's house was like no other that Ray had come across. It comprised a series of large high-ceilinged rooms interconnected by an even larger central room off which all the other rooms opened. Dark timber dominated, on the floor, window frames, built-in furniture and wall mouldings, and all the small windowpane edges were bevelled, leading to rainbows of light projected into the rooms. There was little loose furniture to clutter the spaces. Trevor's parents were much more eccentric than Ray's quite conventional parents and they were secular Jews, not at all religious. They had their own book-lined study rooms in the house and appeared to lead lives rather independently of one another. Trevor had an older sister who, for Ray, oozed sophistication and she initiated the two boys into contemporary music, with Ray particularly pleased to have been introduced to 'Smoke Gets In Your Eyes' sung by The Platters, a velvety sad song of a love that came and then went. But there were many others, like Roy Orbison, Percy Faith, Connie Francis, Elvis Presley, Brenda Lee and the Everly Brothers.

By then Ray had his own small transistor radio and convinced himself of his skill at miming and fully emoting the lyrics while standing in front of the mirror fixed to his wardrobe door. His first mimed success was Roy Orbison's 'Crying', a rich opportunity for expressing adolescent self-pity:

I was alright for a while
I could smile for a while
But I saw you last night,
you held my hand so tight
As you stopped to say, 'Hello'
Oh, you wished me well,
you couldn't tell

That I'd been crying over you
Crying over you
Then you said, 'So long'
Left me standing all alone
Alone and crying
Crying
Crying
Crying

Ray extended his repertoire of mime to include more Roy Orbison songs, 'Blue Bayou' and 'In Dreams', and also songs by Buddy Holly, Elvis, Johnny O'Keefe, The Four Seasons and Cliff Richard.

Cliff Richard

Ray recalls being very chuffed when he attended an event at a local Police and Citizens' Club hall and the sound engineer controlling the music, who had previously worked with well-known bands in England, was taken with what he saw as Ray's physical likeness to Cliff Richard. While chuffed, Ray was never quite convinced of this similarity.

The Beatles and adoring crowds in Melbourne, 1964

And then there was The Beatles, a massive new presence with their captivating music that Ray always found a bit too pretty and contrived. The Beatles toured parts of Australia in the middle of 196 4, excluding Perth, dominating headlines and attracting vast and manic screaming crowds.

There were other English bands like Manfred Mann, Peter and Gordon, and The Shadows. But Ray preferred the tougher R'n'B sound of The Animals and, in particular, their version of 'House of the Rising Sun' and, a bit later, the declamatory and haunting 'We Gotta Get Out of this Place'. This song expressed the beginnings of his own desire to be elsewhere, away from what he saw increasingly as suburban blandness. But Ray's teenage angst seemed petty when he came to understand in time that this song was, for obvious reasons, like an anthem for the US and Australian soldiers during the Vietnam War:

> *We gotta get out of this place*
> *If it's the last thing we ever do*
> *We gotta get out of this place*
> *'Cause girl, there's a better life for me and you.*

Ray's family continued to attend the Shul on Jewish festivals, all dressed up, with his mother sporting her distinctive Shul perfume, but Ray chose to abstain. His overly optimistic parents always tried to coax him along and to reintegrate him into the community, and because he did not comply, his siblings resented him, regarding him as wayward and unfairly privileged. Ray did, however, continue to participate in the numerous food-based celebrations associated with the festivals that were held either at their or a relative's home. For him this was an entirely secular interest, driven by his love of the food rather than a love of the religious rituals or, in some instances, of his relatives.

Ray did not have any real Jewish friends at school apart from Trevor, and theirs was an intermittent friendship based on the closeness of their houses and their mutual desire to be conspirators. They could concoct the most appalling mischief in class, usually prompted by boredom and lack of respect for the teacher. Their most modest attack was the slow but noisy tearing of paper under the desk while their faces conveyed total rapt attention to what the teacher was saying. Their most contrived attacks occurred as a result of their occasional after-school workshops, during which they performed operations on sticks of chalk. They worked out how to clamp the sticks gently into a vice and then, using a drill stand with an appropriate size bit, carefully drill out almost the full length of the chalk stick and, in the narrow tube of space created, insert a variety of fillers. There were the hard fillers like a nail or a screw, and there were the soft, messy fillers like honey or tea leaves. After the fillers were in place, the end of the chalk stick was carefully closed up with a mix of the chalk dust from the drilling operation and white woodworking glue. Then, before the teacher arrived, the doctored chalk sticks were placed in the chalk tray at the base of the class blackboards. It was only a matter of time before the teacher picked up one of these chalk sticks and, on using it, had it disintegrate in their hand, for example, into a splotch of honey smeared down the board. The particular teacher who was the target of this villainy was driven gravely to distraction but, such was the artfulness of Trevor and Ray, he never discovered the culprits, the cause of his ongoing misery.

There were other teachers who engaged the boys and were not subjected to disrespectful treatment. There was the English literature teacher, Mr Gale, who always arrived late to school, in a seriously dishevelled and stained suit, still in his slippers, dropped off by his wife and their large posse of small children who overflowed noisily from the car windows. Students in the classrooms that flanked the driveway loop to the school's entrance were regular witnesses to this spectacle. Despite his lack of personal organisational skills, Mr Gale had the ability to bring a piece of literature vividly to life and to engage even the most sceptical and resistant of students. For Ray, Mr Gale was responsible for making Shakespeare comprehensible and alluring; for presenting Dickens as the great storyteller; and for introducing him to wonderful books outside the school syllabus, like Catcher in the Rye.

Mount Lawley High School was the school where new processes for teaching mathematics were developed, with the students becoming unsuspecting guinea pigs for the state Education Department. This experiment worked for Ray, with previously opaque mathematical equations now made self-evident through a process of reordering and regrouping numbers. To top it off, the team of maths teachers who ran the program were what appeared to be a special breed of tall and highly attractive clever women who all had beautiful legs and always wore high heels to show these legs in their best light. You did not mess with this team of intellectual and physical Amazons.

Having spent three years in a school with no girls, Ray felt uncertain about how to engage with the girls in his class. Nevertheless, he quickly discovered that he preferred the company of girls to boys, and that in his view they were the superior gender, were more mature, more reasonable, more humorous and more beautiful than boys, but, too often, his engagements with them were disturbed by romantic imaginings.

Ray had brief crushes on girls in his classes, with the out-of-reach girls always the most attractive. Despite Ray's Faustian deal with his parents, they remained hopeful that they would, one day, have Jewish grandchildren and there was ongoing pressure on him to satisfy these expectations. There was one Jewish girl he liked very much, but she was way out of his league: tall, slim and elegant, highly intelligent, Ray contrived every now and again to walk home from school with her, but he knew that her circle of admirers was at least two years older than him and far more worldly. There was another Jewish girl who Ray liked.

Donna came to the school on exchange for one term from the USA and, apart from looking like a Jewish version of Annette Funicello, had the sweetest disposition and just enough of the exotic to make her appealing to Ray. They had similar interests and emerging opinions about their worlds, and talked very easily together. Her New York accent was so captivating that Ray could have happily listened to her talk all day. It was a sad day for Ray when her term of exchange came to an end and she had to pack up and leave Perth. A big party was thrown by her Mount Lawley hosts on Donna's last night and she and Ray disappeared for an hour to enjoy some memorable time alone. They did write letters to one another but, such are the distractions of the young, this lasted for only a short while. But to Ray, the other Jewish girls at the school were like mishpocha: extended family, known and without intrigue.

Ray found the Greek girls at the school the most alluring: while there was much about them that was familiar, that was like Jewish girls, there was more that was not, making them, to him, a bit of a mystery. There was, however, one Greek girl with whom Ray had ongoing disagreements of temperament and, too often, was seated next to by the unkind chemistry teacher. She got under his skin, everything about her irritated him and he did all he could to avoid her.

Ray recalls being caned for what was regarded as sacrilege in a religion class. Although there were many Jewish students at the school, all students were bundled in together for religious instruction and it was mistakenly assumed that all had a knowledge of the New Testament. The religion instructor was introducing, as an example of Christ's miraculous powers, a lesson from the Bible and Ray laughed loudly, thinking the story was particularly far-fetched. The teacher was furious and responded cruelly.

At Mount Lawley, the cane was administered to the palm of the hand with, as at the College, the number of strokes determined by the severity of the misdemeanour. Although the religion instructor had regarded Ray's laughter as particularly sinful, the deputy head whose responsibilities included the issuing of corporal punishment, evidently had a different view and dispensed a perfunctory single stroke of the cane.

Ray continued with his segregated art classes and his art work continued to develop. One work of still life rendered in charcoal and chalk, and featuring a large bovine skull, won a statewide student art competition. Ray did not think this was his best work and didn't tell his parents of this success, prompting Joe, when he did find out, to remark of Ray: 'He's too modest, that boy.' In his art work, what Ray was more interested in was cartooning, caricature and the prospect of becoming a latter-day Paul Rigby. Understanding this ambition, Joe pulled some RSL strings and arranged a visit for Ray to the Daily News and an audience with the great Rigby. It was like going to the holy grail. Ray pored over the details of Rigby's workspace – the angle-poise lamp, the size and tilt of his drawing board, the way his paper was taped to the drawing board, the type of paper he used, the pens and the brushes, and the little practice drawings and scribbles on the side. Rigby had a twinkle to his eyes, a smile always flickering across his mouth, and the desire to be constantly witty. Ray felt daunted by his sophistication and skills.

As a corrective follow-up to the magical hour with Paul Rigby, Joe arranged for another visit, this time with the family's bank manager – the big guns were being deployed. The bank manager had been fully briefed by Joe and he played his part as a pragmatic spoiler by advising Ray that there was only one Paul Rigby, that the income of a would-be cartoonist would be precarious at the best, and that Ray really should look for a career that was able to combine his creative interests with something more practical and more able to generate an income. He suggested that studying to become an architect would fit the bill. Ray had always enjoyed building houses from his Bilda-brix construction set and bigger structures from his Meccano set, so the deflecting suggestion was astutely targeted and fell on receptive ground.

At the crime scene, Cooke showing a detective how he shot a victim

On his walks between home and school, Ray had looked with an admiring eye at the modern houses that were built in Coolbinia during the 1950s and 60s. He had several relatives who lived in houses like this and Ray always enjoyed visiting them, not because of affection for those relatives but because he could spend time in the houses. And he did wonder how they came into being, how they were designed to have continuous space that flowed from one area into another and then to the outside. Ray was well primed for the bank manager's prompting.

And yet, a key part of the attraction of these modern houses, the ease of movement and connection between inside and outside, had been closed off as the result of a recent spate of apparently random murders in Perth. The previous habits of an easy, trusting way of life, of not locking doors and windows, of keeping keys in cars, and of sleeping on the lawn and verandas on hot summer nights, had now all been foreclosed. Fear and suspicion gripped Perth as the murderer used a variety of means to kill: there were hit-and-runs in stolen cars, stabbings, strangulations and shootings. Speculation about the murderer and motives dominated casual conversations. The first murders were of young women in affluent suburbs and then, on Australia Day in 1963, five people were shot across the suburbs of Perth, with two dying from their wounds. Eight people were killed over a four-year period until the police laid a cunning trap after a rifle found hidden in bushes proved to be one of the weapons used in the killings. A replica rifle was placed back in the bushes and the police lay in wait until Eric Edgar Cooke returned to the vacant block to retrieve his hidden rifle.

Once arrested he admitted to the murders and, in a bizarrely documented display, he took police to the crime scenes, demonstrating where and how he had conducted his murders. Thirteen months after his arrest and following a brief trial, Eric Edgar Cooke became the last person to be executed in Western Australia. He was hanged in Fremantle Prison at 8am on 26 October 1964. Ray remembers the day as being quiet and sombre as the sentence was carried out and the prison doctor's pronouncement of death was made.

Ray always attempted to get work in the long break between the school years — it got him out into the world and it earned him some useful money. At the end of his third year of high school he worked as a packer and delivery boy for a wholesaler who sold hair products to hairdressing salons for women. The owner was a friend of

The delivery boy

Joe and Ethel's, a member of the Jewish community, and sympathetic to the need to bring Ray back to the fold. Yet, instead of responding to the frequent sermonising directed to him at work, Ray had great fun being teased by and flirting with the young female hairdressers.

At the end of fourth year his job was to clean out the roof space of an old factory that made component parts for gas and electric stoves. Although the pay was good, this job was no fun – it was filthy and very hot in the roof space, and he had to carry heavy stove parts down steep ladders. After work he sometimes joined others from the factory at the nearby beach, swimming away the discomforts of the job. On these occasions, there was sexual banter and tension, with couples heading off to the sandhills for lusty trysts, although Ray was not yet an initiate.

Ray's earlier exposure to the South Fremantle Football Club left him with an enduring interest in the game of Australian Rules. As we observed earlier, while he was a capable performer at kick-to-kick and marking contests, he had

Mount Lawley High School Rugby Team, 1965

little capacity to read the play during a game. So, with encouragement from the rugby coach based on his evident bulk, his Jumbo-ness, rather than non-evident skills, Ray switched to Rugby Union as his winter sport at school. He became a hulking forward who, over time, moved through the scrum, initially as a prop, then a second rower, and finishing as the lock in the school team. The team was blessed with the presence of a recent English immigrant who became a student at Mount Lawley High, a boy who played like a will-o'-the-wisp genius. Timothy was born to play rugby and was highly skilled with his side-steps, his fend-offs, his tackling, his passing, and his ability to score tries. With him as their leading player, Mount Lawley became the top team in the high school competition.

Ray's contribution was usually serviceable as the go-to player in the line-out and as a bullocking member of the scrum – but he did play one very good game. In this game, he completely controlled the line-outs, he carried the ball often and broke defensive lines, and he scored two tries. This was the first and second, which would also be the last, time ever that he carried the ball over the line to score a try. It so happened that this game was played in front of the selector for the state schoolboy team and Ray's performance was sufficiently impressive to get him into the state team that went to Adelaide and competed in the schoolboy rugby carnival between the states. Because of the dominance of the Mount Lawley team in the competition, six of their members were selected for the Western Australian team of 24.

Ray as touring rugby player with his fellow Mount Lawley High School state representatives

Ray posing in his rugby gear

This was Ray's first time out of Western Australia, his first flight in an aeroplane and, apart from the Pemberton school camp, his first extended time away from his parents, leaving him highly excited. He was billeted in a house in Morphettville with a kind family of rugby enthusiasts who couldn't do enough to make him feel at home. Ray was intrigued by the differences he noticed in the billeting house from what had become familiar to him at his parents' home. These differences were most evident in the household smells – the soap, the toilet deodorant, the washing detergent used for bedsheets and towels, the cooking, and the sweetly scented aftershave used by the man-of-the-house. But the differences were also obvious in the absences – no mezuzahs, no menora, no tchotchkes that referred to the holy land, and no Friday night blessings for the coming sabbath.

Sadly, Ray did not repeat his very good game that earned him state selection and, despite the presence of the brilliant Timothy, the Western Australian team did not win any of their five games. Theirs was the least developed of the rugby-playing states in Australia and it showed. It was a glum flight back to Perth.

In summer, Ray attempted to play cricket and he made his 'school house' team as a middling batsman, a medium-pace bowler of no distinction, and an enthusiastic fielder who could not throw the ball very far. The earlier fantasy cricket forays with Wally had left Ray ill-prepared for the real thing. His most memorable cricket event proved to be extremely painful. It was usual practice when training in the cricket nets to wear a 'box', a hard plastic protector worn over the vulnerable genitals. Showing unwise bravado, Ray chose not to wear a 'box' during one training session. When it was his turn to bat, the bowlers were rotated and Ray had to face up to the impressive Bob Massie. Massie went on to become a test bowler for Australia, capable of bowling fast and swinging deliveries.

The first ball bowled to Ray was safely outside the off stump and although he took a big swipe at the ball, Ray was nowhere near connecting with it. The next ball was a bit shorter and aimed more at the stumps and Ray, in a brazen show of misplaced confidence in his abilities, attempted to hook it out to mid-wicket. He opened up his stance by taking his left leg across to give him room to make the shot. But all that happened was that he exposed his unprotected genitals to the trajectory of the ball that, again, he completely missed. The ball did not miss him. Ray collapsed in incandescent pain and had to be helped to the embankment behind the nets where he was left to recover. Being hit in the balls was cause for collective mirth rather than concern and sympathy, and this was how Ray's agonising plight was treated by the other students at the nets. It took Ray what seemed to be hours before he was capable of staggering away from where he lay and then many days before the pain and swelling eased. Ray's cricketing career was, from that point, over.

Ray and organised sports were never easy bedfellows and this experience hastened their separation. He was more comfortable playing the fool, hamming it up in school 'reviews' held at the end of each term. The presence of an appreciative audience was a great stimulant for Ray and his timing, his assumed accents, and his character exaggerations became honed with audience encouragement. He enjoyed the process of co-writing scripts, of designing and making minimal sets, and then co-directing and acting the skits that focused on school incidents and newsworthy events. And, to his surprise, he found he enjoyed co-writing with the Greek girl he had attempted to avoid in chemistry classes. When the two of them re-met after many, many years, they got on like a house on fire, sharing values across culture, politics and life in general.

Ray gained some notoriety within the school from his involvement in the reviews, sufficient to have him elected as a school prefect in his final year, against all his own expectations and desires. The best part about being a prefect was enjoying the company of the girl prefects, including three of the beguiling Greek girls, during the regular meetings that overflowed with self-importance.

As he matured, Ray was changing, becoming less the well-behaved, responsible and jovial teenager and more of the young dissident, argumentative and disagreeable, cranky about any imposed authority and fascinated, occasionally obsessed, by the promise of full-on sex. He had less to do with his family, spending most of his time at home closed up in his bedroom, prompting his siblings to place a sign on his door that read STAR BOARDER. In this cranky and defiant mode he teamed up with Antonio Cappelletti,

Mount Lawley High School Prefects, 1965

son of Italian immigrants, and a cavalier mutineer who was fun and dangerous to be with. He and Ray enjoyed provoking people, flirting with girls, and generally getting into mischief. They spent a lot of time together laughing, often at the expense of others. Later in life, when he saw Federico Fellini's film I Vitelloni, Ray recognised he and Antonio as being like the aimless larrikins in the film, a two-person troublesome rat pack.

Ray was to suffer another near-death experience while at high school. He and Antonio decided to wag school on a day of classes they considered boring and hitchhike to Scarborough Beach. Scarborough was the wildest of Perth's many beaches that were strung out along the edge of the Indian Ocean. It was the home of the 'Snakepit', a dance bar for bodgies and widgies right on the beach; it was the favoured beach of the fearsome motorbike gangs; it had a wide and straight sand strip before you hit the water; it had big, powerful long waves and the water quickly deepened as the sand fell away. It was not a place for the faint-hearted. Ray had been there many times to swim, to be sprayed with oil to prompt a tan on his white Ashkenazi skin that only ever became sunburned, to watch the bathing beauty parades, and to roam through the adjacent sand dunes looking for signs of life and love.

The Snake Pit, Scarborough Beach

The waves could be high and ferocious, often ending as 'dumpers', churning swimmers around underwater and leaving them gasping for air. Ray loved to bodysurf the big waves for long distances, feeling as if he was flying. He considered himself a reasonably strong swimmer, having achieved his bronze medallion in lifesaving classes and competing for his schools in swimming events. But Scarborough was always a test.

The day that Ray and Antonio wagged school turned out to be sunny but blustery, keeping numbers on the beach to only a few. Ray ran straight into the surging sea while Antonio, more circumspectly, spread his towel and lay on the sand to soak up some sun. As soon as Ray swam up to the breakers he knew something was not at all right. He was caught in a powerful rip that quickly took him out beyond the waves and to the dark sea. As he had been taught, he tried to swim across the rip, parallel to the shore, but was pushed further out. Ray knew he had to keep calm – but it was hard to stay calm when the shore was getting further and further away. Ray decided he better put his arm up in the air to seek help, but he knew there was little likelihood there would be anyone on the shore who could see him. As his arm frantically waved, Ray could only think of what his mother would say when she learned that her first-born son had drowned while wagging school! The shame of it...He had that often-described sensation of his life flashing before his eyes, experiences compressed into a jumble of emotions, a kind of colour movie that was made up of highlights of his short life. Was this punishment for having turned his back on the Jewish God? And then, when he had just about given up hope, a miracle: Ray was grabbed under the arms by a surfer who must have seen him in trouble and paddled across the rip to help him. Ray remembers the surfer as a big strong man and he hauled Ray onto his long surfboard.

Before he knew it, Ray was back on shore, exhausted, weak and so grateful. But before he could properly thank the surfer he and his board had taken once more to the waves. Ray was now some distance from where Antonio was still sunbathing on the beach and, after catching his breath, he staggered off along the soft white sand to reach him.

Ray and his rescuing surfer

Antonio was entirely oblivious to Ray's escapade and, for a while, refused to believe it. When he did accept what had happened, Antonio offered no sympathy but, instead, laughed and laughed. Annoyed with him, Ray left the beach and hitched home alone, sheepishly sneaking in and showering before joining the family for dinner. Nothing was said about this misadventure although, that night, Ray was unusually chatty.

Ray did not include Antonio, or anyone else that he knew, in his covert attendance of dance classes. He learned about the venue and its offerings from Trevor's sister when, after the three of them had listened to some music together, she described how she had become a good dancer. Every Wednesday he wore slightly more dapper clothes than usual and, after school, caught a bus into the city. He walked up Murray Street until he reached the doorway and stairs that took him up to the dance studio and its vast floor of scuffed timber boards. The high ceiling with its exposed timber trusses had suspended fans whirring above the dance floor and skylights that allowed in bright shafts of late afternoon sunshine. Music was played either from an old upright piano with its front panel removed, or from a portable record player with scratchy sound.

Ray was interested in learning to dance to help him become the suave young-man-about-town. He was also hoping to meet girls and, in particular, the girl-of-his-dreams – she was a loner like him, beautiful and mysterious, an urban sophisticate able to dance with elan the rumba, samba, waltz and quickstep. These were the dance styles Ray learned with passing competence – but he never could get the moves right to be any good at jiving. Alas, the girl-of-his-dreams must have attended a different dance class, because she was not at this one. Instead, there were many late-adolescent males like him, pimply, smelly, gormless, all hoping that dance would transform them into dashing young men. And there were older men and women, lonely and looking for partners, and the odd couple who were accomplished dancers, impressing all with their command of the dance floor.

Ray's school subjects were all manageable for him. Chemistry was a pain and held no interest but, with a bit of work, it could be learned. He wisely pulled out of French a year earlier because he found it unreasonably difficult and had been singled out repeatedly by the teacher for his appalling pronunciation and obvious lack of homework on conjugating verbs. Often, the teacher made him sit at her table at the front of the class where she could intimidate and direct him as she thought was needed. Ray convinced himself that she had a crush on him.

It has to be said that Ray was never a great student. He was content to cruise at a comfortable level of engagement that did not require too much study, confident that his savviness, his 'shitty-shrewdness', would prevail and save the day. His parents did not share Ray's confidence and, instead, they recognised a looming missed chance for Ray to score highly in what was then called the Leaving Certificate, with the score giving access to university courses. So they commissioned a study adviser to visit with them and Ray at their house one evening. This earnest adviser established a set of protocols with Ray where he was to work on a single topic for no more than 30 minutes. After summarising what he had learned, he was then to take a break, what Ray thought the adviser called to becoming an architect. He had carried out some basic research and decided he liked what he saw of the profession: the different sizes of offices from one person to huge; the international transportability of the skills; the designing of a range of building types; the potential to make a positive contribution to society; and the fact that it was a profession where creativity and 'style' were important. Leaping optimistically ahead, Ray decided that, once he was an architect, he would purchase an Alfa Romeo GTV, and he placed a picture of the elegant but unflashy car, in pale blue, on his pin-up board to help propel this ambition.

This new commitment resulted in Ray becoming more serious about studying for his Leaving. His 'mock' Leaving results had been inauspicious and, as a result, he now spent many late nights reading and summarising into note form, finally getting into the swing and routine of studying. Ray recalls Joe getting up from his bed late one night when Ray was making a snack to help keep himself going. Joe growled disbelievingly: 'You don't make toast at two o'clock in the morning!' But Ray's efforts paid off and his results were sufficiently good to win a scholarship, a cadetship and access to the architecture course. Because it paid better, Ray chose the cadetship over the scholarship, choosing not to give any thought to the five-year bond that required cadets to work for the government following completion of their studies. He decided that the long holiday that followed the exams was going to be a really good one, celebrating a job well done. He was now absolutely trouble-free, and it was a time for earning a bit of money and having fun before starting his new studies.

Ray applied for and was given a job on the Coca-Cola trucks as a swamper for eight weeks. The swamper was there as the driver's assistant in the busy summer months and helped unload and deliver crates with full bottles of drink, and then load the empty crates and bottles from the place of delivery. The trucks would start loading early in the morning, in the crisp cool air, deliver their first load and then return to the factory to be loaded up for the next delivery that day. Ray got to see parts of Perth that he did not know existed, and they regularly travelled out to places beyond the metropolitan area. The trucks drove long distances over the day, leaving a lot of time for cabin chatting with the driver. In this way, Ray's local knowledge expanded, both in terms of geography and 'blokey' life.

To each load would be added a free crate of family-size bottles of Coca-Cola for the driver and swamper. They swapped these hot bottles for cold ones to quench their thirst, or swapped them for food when hungry. Ray did the lion's share of shifting both the full and the empty bottles, clambering up the truck to retrieve the full crates and loading them on his barrow. He became quite skilled and speedy and prided himself on the fact that, unlike his driver, he never had a barrow spill. While Ray did this heavy labour, his driver chatted up the female shop assistants and took care of the paperwork. Ray sweated buckets and, as a result, drank a huge amount of the free Coca-Cola each day. Although only seventeen, Ray was paid as an adult and earned quite a stash.

There was an unfortunate legacy to this work. When Ray next went for a dental check-up, his regular dentist recoiled in horror when he looked into Ray's mouth: 'What have you DONE to your teeth? You've ruined them!' The dentist put the damage down to the massive consumption of Coca-Cola and the amount of sugar carried by the drink. Ray ended up with a mouth full of amalgam fillings.

Following the swamping work and now well cashed-up, Ray spent two weeks at Rottnest with a schoolmate and his family. This mate, Phil Cox, had been Ray's fellow second-rower in the Mount Lawley High School rugby scrum and both of them had opted to study architecture and both had been offered cadetships by the state government. They were joined by the hips in the rugby scrum and looked like being similarly joined in architecture for the next decade or so. Phil and his family were Rottnest veterans, holidaying there for a month every summer and staying in the same bungalow on Thomson Bay. Rottnest is a small publicly owned island eighteen kilometres off the coast from Fremantle. It is a beautiful island of rocky limestone outcrops, picturesque bays with glorious beaches and inland lakes, and is the habitat of a unique animal called the quokka, a small hopping marsupial after which the island was named in 1696 by Willem de Vlamingh, the early Dutch explorer: 't Eylandt 't Rottenest (Rats' Nest Island).

Quokka

Rottnest has a dark history, being used by the early European settlers as a prison island for Aboriginal people, with a large number of those imprisoned dying on the island from disease, mistreatment or by hanging. Some visitors to the island claim to sense strongly the past misery of the place and will not return.

This was Ray's second holiday stint with Phil and his family at Rottnest and he was looking forward immensely to a repeat of the daily patterns he learned during the first stint. In addition, this family was devoid of any religious allegiance or imperative, a respite for Ray. The days at Rottnest started at sunrise with Phil and Ray heading off on their bikes for an early morning swim at the Basin and a snorkel around the reefs, combined with checking and emptying the cray pots that Phil's father had placed in his favoured spots in the nearby bays.

The smaller crays were cooked and eaten while the larger crays were kept in safe pots in Thomson Bay for taking

The Basin at Rottnest Island

home. On returning to the bungalow, Phil's mother would make breakfast: sometimes it was white Rottnest Bakery bread, fried in dripping, but usually it was pan-fried herring or garfish, caught, cleaned and butterflied the day before. A short sleep after breakfast compensated for the early start to the day and helped with staying up late at night. A bike ride through the settlement and out for a swim to a distant bay cultivated an appetite for lunch. Sometimes these rides went as far as the West End to watch the ever-present pod of surfing dolphins, or to the Oliver Hill gun battery, a remnant unused protector from WWII.

Crayfish, forbidden to Ray by Jewish dietary laws, simply prepared or in a mornay, was a regular lunch, together with an illicit beer. At that time, the legal age for drinking alcohol was 21. This, however, did not stop the mature-looking seventeen-year-olds Ray and Phil heading to the Rottnest Arms for afternoon beers. At holiday times, the bar was so crowded that the boys were not asked for proof of age – and the small local police force had better things to do than check under-age drinking on an island where there were no private cars and therefore no danger from drunk drivers.

Late afternoon was the time for fishing and Phil's father, normally a reclusive and sardonic presence, transformed to become a vital single-minded leader of fishing missions. For weeks before the Rottnest holidays he farmed a vast collection of wriggling maggots to be used for bait. He also had his own refined recipe for a burley mix. Both the burley and maggots worked a treat and, as a result of this tutelage, Ray has never since been a more successful fisherman. Where they cast their lines and what they fished for depended on the direction of the wind and Phil's father's savviness. Herring was the normal catch but there were also garfish, skippy, silver bream and tailor. The fish were cleaned and readied for cooking as soon as the fishermen returned to the bungalow. There was always a sufficient catch to feed the full family and have some left over for breakfast the next day.

Sunburn cream was unheard of in those days and the sun's toxic work was often abetted by the application of oil to the exposed skin. Sunburn was a constant, worn proudly to proclaim the bearer as an outdoor warrior. Nevertheless, sunburn was painful, eased momentarily by the misguided application of methylated spirits. The burnt skin would often peel off in sheets after a few days, blister in the worst instances, expose new skin and the burning cycle would begin all over again. This careless bravado was to cause uncomfortable problems for both Phil and Ray later in life.

After dinner and then rounds of combative games of cards with the family, Ray and Phil headed off to cruise around the settlement and check out the parties. The settlement was sufficiently small and relaxed to admit party crashers. If there were no parties that attracted them, they ended up at the Rottnest Arms.

During their time at Rottnest, two major events in Australia took place. The first was the resignation of Robert Menzies as Prime Minister of Australia. For all but the first year of Ray's life, Menzies had been PM, and he therefore seemed like a fixture, with the name Menzies synonymous with the role. He was the longest serving of Australia's prime ministers, having held the post over two periods for more than a combined eighteen years. Patrician and conservative, and committed to wearing double-breasted suits, 'Pig Iron Bob' led Australia through the post-war period of growing affluence, with one of his last legacies being the misguided commitment of Australian troops to Vietnam. Menzies was reported as saying at the time of his resignation: 'One becomes tired...' Following Menzies' resignation, Harold Holt, who held the position of Treasurer under Menzies, was elected to lead the Liberal Party. As the new Prime Minister, he formed a new government. Holt was less than two years in the role when he disappeared while swimming in the sea near Portsea in Victoria. He was last seen in rough seas and, because his body was never found, there was ongoing intrigue about what may have happened, including the conspiratorial allegation that he was a spy for another country and had been picked up by their submarine.

The second major event was Australia's currency shifting from the mathematically awkward pound, with its twenty shillings and twelve pence, to become decimal, introducing the dollar and its hundred cents. This ended a long re-education campaign during which the public was invited to suggest names for the new currency. There were some shockers, including austral, boomer, kanga, roo, emu, digger, dinkum and kwid. But the worst had been proposed by Menzies while still Prime Minister: in rejecting all that the public had suggested, he decided on the 'royal', an indication of his ongoing affection for Britain and its monarchy. This clearly offended an emerging strain of republicanism and the protests were sufficiently strong for the royal to be jettisoned in favour of the internationally ubiquitous but bland dollar.

The design for the jettisoned one royal note to replace the ten shilling note

The two weeks at Rottnest passed very quickly and happily. The family pack-up for departure was well practised and very efficient and the full household made their way to the ferry for passage back to Fremantle. In two days time, a still sunburnt Ray and Phil started a new adventure as architecture students at the Perth Technical College. At that time, the PTC was the only institution in Perth that offered formal study in architecture from year one. The University of Western Australia had just started a degree program but it began at third year, requiring students to complete successfully the first two years of study at PTC.

PART **five**

Ray and Phil joined about 120 other first-year architecture students, with very few females as part of that number, all taking a taxing number of units of study. The course was directed towards the acquisition of skills: there were many technical studies subjects together with basic design, history and art. Ray thrived on the atmosphere of the place, its ambition and its demands. And he loved the location. Perth Technical College was in the centre of the city of Perth, on St Georges Terrace. Over the road, and linking to Hay Street, was Zimpel's Arcade in which was located Graham's Coffee Lounge, a meeting place for the architecture students who considered themselves cool and urbane. In addition to passable cappuccinos, Graham's offered what became for Ray a signature lunch dish of toasted ham and tomato sandwiches. They were pressed thin and laced with lots of salt and pepper. There were many department stores and some government offices nearby and all their cafeterias were tested to determine the better ones. There was the Cox Brothers department store cafeteria with its outdoor roof terrace overlooking the busy city corner of Hay and William streets, Boans tea rooms for a bit of old-fashioned decorum, and the internalised cafeterias at Foy and Gibson, David Jones and Aherns, all with their own attributes and specialty dishes for targeting. And when lunches were bought as takeaways they were often eaten on the roof of the Trustees Building next door to the PTC, allowing a bird's-eye view of the city below. There was a remarkable lack of security and lack of concern for safety, allowing Ray and the other lunch-eating students to access the roof and sit on the parapet edge with their legs dangling over. Around the corner, on Mill Street, was the Adelphi Hotel, a favoured meeting and drinking place for the architectural profession. The students approached this Mecca timidly, conscious of their under-drinking-age status, but in awe of those who were actually practising architects and living that life.

Ray and fellow students horsing around at PTC

Theosophical Society in Arundale Hall, Perth (1929, demolished 1981)

The beginning of Ray's first year at PTC coincided with an event that outraged architects across Australia: the forced resignation of Joern Utzon as the architect of the Sydney Opera House. Ray had no awareness of how Utzon had been driven into this position, but he knew of the Opera House and its promise, and he enjoyed the sense of noisy professional camaraderie, united in their indignation, that accompanied his entry into the study of architecture.

Part of the architecture students' program involved crossing the railway line and attending James Street Technical College for drawing classes with the art students. This gave Ray a taste of the alternative direction he could have pursued. This part of the city also introduced him to several institutions that he visited many times over. There were the state institutions – the museum, the art gallery and the library – and there was the intriguing Theosophical Society on Museum Street.

Jiddu Krishnamurti (1895 – 1986)

It attracted a range of eccentric devotees and offered to the public a quirky library and small bookshop dedicated to Theosophy. Here, Ray discovered the writings of Krishnamurti, in whom he became captivated for many years. His book, The First and Last Freedom, became like a bible for Ray, questioning many cultural assumptions, including the basis of belief and truth, and providing for Ray a ready-made justification for his earlier rejection of thedoctrines of Judaism. Little did he know that, later in life, considerations of belief and truth would take on different hues.

The city also provided numerous cinemas, from the grandly decorated picture palaces with giant screens and wondrous sound systems to the small sleazy ones filled by men in raincoats. If there was time between lectures, and often if there was not, Ray would go and see a film, usually with fellow students but sometimes on his own. In addition to popular blockbusters, he saw some memorable arthouse films, including The Collector, in which a butterfly collector's interest takes a sinister turn; The Spy Who Came in from the Cold, a gritty and unromanticised tale of espionage; The Knack...and How to Get It, providing an intoxicating glimpse of a zany swinging London in the 1960s; and Alphaville, a stylish and alarming look at a dystopian future world based solely on science and the rational. There were many others and they contributed to Ray's enduring passion for and growing knowledge of film.

Ray became quite comfortable doing things on his own and going off for small 'adventures'. In addition to film watching, Ray spent time in the basement billiard halls, with their stale interiors dominated by cigarette smoke and the sound of clicking balls, occasionally filling in as a partner for serious players, those who played for money. He never did become adept at billiards or snooker and players never asked him to partner them more than once. Top floors and rooftops provided unique views of the city and Ray always enjoyed testing their accessibility.

Cigarette rolling 'machine'

Another solo adventure of sorts, following the pattern of his covert dance classes the previous year, was attending acting classes. Again, the class venue was accessed up a dark narrow staircase, this time off Cremorne Arcade not far from the PTC. The class was offered by a once-promising local thespian, an older woman whose acting experience appeared to be of the melodramatic variety. Nevertheless, the location and class times suited Ray and he was keen to extend the performance skills that gave him modest public success in the school reviews. He was also keen to meet some new girls. It was only a small group that attended the weekly late afternoon sessions, three girls about his age, an older woman, and a lonely middle-aged man who reeked of body odour and was cripplingly withdrawn. As a result, when they read plays, they often had to perform multiple parts, both male and female. Ray recalls his finest moments being in the role of Heathcliff in an adapted version of Wuthering Heights. Apart from the other male, they all overacted, hamming their way through the part-learned scripts with big gestures and loud voices in unconvincing accents. Ray bailed out after one term, deciding he was not learning anything useful and, besides, none of the girls attracted his interest. His acting ambitions were to lie dormant for a few years before being reactivated at the University Dramatic Society when he shifted his studies to The University of Western Australia.

During his time free of classes, when he was not watching a film or playing billiards badly, Ray also attended trials at the Supreme Court. He would sit alone in what he remembers as the austere steeply raked upstairs public gallery and marvel at the arcane procedures of the court and the usually astonishing, frequently tragic, foibles on trial. While fascinated by the gravity and theatre of it all, he was at no stage remotely interested in switching courses to study law.

Ray marvelled at the powerful effect of the Supreme Court Building, a grand neo-classical edifice that proclaimed emphatically the status and role of the law in society, and that made the individual feel small and ephemeral next to its scale and enduring qualities. Adding to its external impact, the interior was no less daunting. For Ray it was

The Supreme Court Building, Perth

an early lesson in the impact architecture could have on people. The high entrance, the impressive stairs, the dark polished timber wall linings, the wigged and severe judge sitting up high above the floor where the action took place, the sombre, sober and formal proceedings, and the passing of sentences all seemed highly theatrical – but all too real in the way it affected lives.

The walk along St Georges Terrace between the Perth Technical College and the Supreme Court took Ray past four city blocks of office buildings, richly ornamented buildings that dated from the late nineteenth to early twentieth centuries. Among them was a quite distinctive building type which was accessed by climbing a half flight of stairs from the footpath to a modest-sized but well-finished lobby space. The timber, metal and stone detailing was rich and artisan-like in its making. The old lifts were a treat, double-layered doors, brass or bronze, with detailed infill stone and woodwork. They lacked the precision and smooth workings of more modern lifts but were a great pleasure to use. Half a flight down from the footpath were small convenience shops – coffee and tea, hats, tobacco, drycleaners, newsagents – accessed by sometimes winding stairs, narrower than the main entry stairs.

This urbane and characteristic building type has now all but disappeared from the streets of Perth, to be replaced, in Ray's view, by characterless buildings controlled by changed planning regulations, propelled by motivations of profit that overpower those of civic contribution, and producing an outcome that could be found in many second-rate cities of the world.

Believing it to be a sign of sophistication, and because there was no discouragement from his parents, both of whom smoked, Ray took up cigarettes and became familiar with Perth's specialist tobacconists and their more exotic merchandise. He liked the assumed glamour of the Sobranie Black Russian cigarettes, the aroma of the stumpy fat Gauloises and the restrained quality of Senior Service. But he settled on carrying a pack of filterless Chesterfields or Camels, depending on availability, together with a pouch of Drum and rolling papers. He later refined this to just the Drum and a metal rolling machine in which he could carry the tobacco and papers. He loved this compact kit and the deft orderly ritual involved with making a cigarette.

When he first started at the PTC, Ray would get himself to the city by using buses or by hitchhiking. When he needed a car to go to the beach, to parties, or to take out a girl, he borrowed his parents' car. But borrowing the car came with a caveat. If he was taking out a Jewish girl, the car was freely his, no question; if not, then no go. After a while, and after numerous lies to his parents about who accompanied him in the car, Ray decided he needed to buy his own car. He found a 1954 Volkswagen Beetle with a small rear window and this became the car he had to have. It boasted a serviceable motor, was a kind of jungle-green colour and had a number of dents. Ray and Wayne, another architecture student friend who lived nearby and was a car enthusiast, filled and sanded the dents and prepared the car for eventual repainting. Wayne's father managed a vehicle body shop and, against his better judgement, arranged for the repaint in a bright yellow selected by Ray, the unmissable safety colour used by the Department of Civil Aviation. The VW now looked

Ray with his VW

very sharp. Ray had to work every Saturday morning in his parents' shop to repay the $400 he borrowed to pay for the car. After several years operating their newsagency and gift shop on William Street in the city, Ray's parents sold up and leased a newsagency/stationery shop in front of a barber on Hay Street near Milligan Street. Another component of the lease was a small magic shop in the same building but separated from the newsagency by the front entry and stairs to a boarding house above, which had many colourful tenants. Ray worked in the magic shop, an Aladdin's cave of junk trickery that included plastic vomits and dog poos, whoopee cushions, and a selection of zombie and other masks. It was not a job that tested him and he spent most of his time there flirting with the full-time young saleswoman.

Ray was surprised by the reaction of some members of the Jewish community to his Volkswagen. Understandably, with so few years since the end of World War II, the resentment felt towards anything German remained very strong. But Ray did wonder whether the ire was directed to the outrageous yellow colour of his car or to him as a self-declared outsider, rather than its manufacturing roots, as many Jewish people he knew drove Mercedes.

The VW was very basic and had no fuel gauge, only a lever that allowed activation of a small reserve tank when the main tank ran out of fuel. Unfortunately, Ray could never remember whether the lever had been previously activated, so the car regularly ran out of fuel, necessitating the carrying of a spare can of fuel.

The car allowed Ray a level of freedom he hadn't previously enjoyed. If he felt like going for a drive, he didn't have to ask anyone, he could just get his keys and head off – wherever. He remembers that sense of freedom being heightened whenever he drove along Thomas Street on summer evenings, all windows open, the wild bush of Kings Park on his left, with the inexplicable smell of cut watermelon as the herald of a night of pleasure, and the heady prospect of meeting new young people all looking to have a good time.

Shortly after Ray bought his car, he recalls answering the front doorbell and finding Phil looking distressed. Phil never just dropped in like this, and Ray thought that something must be wrong. Phil then described how, two nights before, he had been a passenger in Rob Courtney's car, an old Holden, and they'd had an accident on Green Street, coming back from Scarborough. Rob was one of those people for whom the gods had been smiling when he was born – he was a strikingly good-looking young man with a warm heart and a good sense of humour. He had also been part of the school rugby scrum with Ray and Phil.

The accident hadn't seemed too bad, Phil was badly jolted but unhurt, and he described looking across at Rob in the driver's seat and realising he was unconscious. Although he did not have a scratch on his body, tragically, Rob had been killed by the impact with his steering wheel. This was, for both Ray and Phil, the first death of a peer they had experienced and, apart from the deep sadness of it, it provided a stark reminder about their callowness as drivers and the fragility of life

Nevertheless, shortly after the accident, Phil bought an old VW. Not as old as Ray's, it had a large rear window and boasted a fuel gauge together with other improvements. Ray and Phil continued their Rottnest pattern at night, going out looking for parties and, later with Wayne, to nightclubs and getting to know the local music scene. The Trendsetter and The Beach House became the preferred clubs because their regular band was the Beat'n Tracks, highly skilled at covers of Spencer Davis, Motown and blues artists, Cream, Small Faces, The Animals and other bands that Ray liked.

Because they were such regulars, Ray, Phil and Wayne got to know the band, their manager Peter Andrew, and his contingent of stylish friends. After the Trendsetter gigs, they would, every so often, all decamp to the Hole-in-the-Wall Club, a theatre with an early morning bar and meeting place for musicians and their hangers-on. With his limited experience of the world, Ray felt that the Hole-in-the-Wall Club was the epicentre of urban sophistication.

Alice

During one of their nights out, Phil showed Ray a small photograph of a girl he had met at a party some months earlier. He explained that he really liked this girl and was looking forward to her return from a year in Paris, an end-of-school trip organised by the private school she had attended. Little did Ray understand at that time the effect this girl, whose name was Alice, would have on his life.

Bob Dylan in 1966

Another event that affected his life occurred on 23 April 1966 when Bob Dylan played a concert at the Capitol Theatre in Perth and to which Ray was offered a ticket. This was Ray's first visit to the Capitol and the first time he had attended a concert alone. This was also Dylan's first visit to Australia and the first tour where he was backed by an electric band, the Hawks, later to become The Band. For Ray, Dylan really struck a powerful chord – he left the concert elated, feeling an uncanny connection with the music. Dylan's songs and his way of singing somehow meshed with Ray's own still-forming response to the world, and his music proved to be a lifelong passion.

The Capitol Theatre on William Street, with the Embassy Ballroom next door, upstairs in Temple Court

He also fell in love with the grand and quirky theatre, with its highly textured exuberant exterior and its magical art nouveau-inspired interiors covered in murals of painted nature. He'd not seen anything like this before and found it exhilarating. He was inspired to research the building, discovering that it was designed by the eminent local architect George Temple Poole, in partnership with Christian Frederik Mouritzen. It opened in 1929 with the promise that it was 'Dedicated to the better entertainment of Perth'. Ray was dismayed when, two years after the Dylan concert, the Capitol was demolished during a period of urban expansion mayhem, fuelled by mineral wealth, when a number of highly distinctive buildings in Perth made way for tall office buildings of little distinction.

Later that year the annual convention of the Australian Architecture Students' Association was held in Perth. Students from all around Australia gathered on the leafy campus of the Claremont Teachers' College to attend talks by a quite astonishing group of international luminaries. Heading the list was Richard Buckminster Fuller, the American architect, inventor and futurist who was prophetic in his concern for protecting spaceship Earth. He developed the geodesic dome, a structure that contained maximum volume by minimal means, and, later, was instrumental in developing the Whole Earth Catalog, a compendium for survival on Earth, acknowledged by Steve Jobs as an early version of Google.

Ray recalls 'Bucky's' conference address as being hours in length and him understanding very little of it, but nevertheless, realising he was attending something quite special. There was also Jacob Bakema and Aldo van Eyck from the Netherlands, John Voelcker from the UK, and Paul Ritter, who had recently arrived in Perth to take up the City Planner role for the City of Perth. Between the formal talks, the visitors relaxed by chatting with the students on the buffalo grass under the bright Perth sun.

This was heady stuff for a first-year student and the most evident legacy was the local experimentation with geodesic domes. Even Ray built a basic dome from struts made of conduits short enough to fit under the bonnet of his VW, simple ply connector hubs with bolts, and a black and clear plastic covering cut and taped to fit over the structure when erected. This served as quick shelter for all sorts of needs.

To coincide with the convention, the students arranged their annual T-Square Ball, a festive dressy event held at the Embassy Ballroom, next door to the Capitol Theatre in the city. Ray recalls learning with pleasure that the Beat'n Tracks were to be the featured band. They performed with their usual great energy and skill, and everyone was having a very fine time. Midway through the event, Ray saw, in this packed and lively setting, a familiar older man who lived around the corner from him in Coolbinia. He was the father of two attractive girls who had gone to Mount Lawley High School with Ray, and this unlikely presence was darting anxiously in and out of the groups of partying people as if desperately looking for someone. It was later that evening that Ray learned the terrible news that there had been an accident at a railway crossing approaching Perth and that a car with a group of architecture students from New South Wales had been hit by a train. With these students, all coming to the T-Square Ball, was one of the Coolbinia man's daughters and, tragically, she had been killed in the collision. It seems that he had heard about the crash from a radio bulletin and, being overcome by a ghastly intuition, rushed in panic to the Embassy Ballroom to look, in vain, for his now dead daughter.

Not long after, Ray had another one of his adolescent brushes with death when, driving his VW one wet morning, his brakes failed. In an instinctive reaction to the car in front of him braking and, alarmingly, not getting any response from his own brake pedal, he tugged at the hand brake and was sent into a wild spin on the slippery road. As had happened with the close call on his bicycle when he first rode it to high school, the car arced through oncoming traffic, miraculously finding its own safe path, and ended up almost perfectly parked on the other side of the street, facing in the direction opposite to which he had been travelling. Again, death was not yet ready for Ray.

This moment of danger, this spinning out of control, is where we take our leave from the boy we selected in the 1956 North Perth Primary School class photograph, from Ray and his transition from cossetted Jewish schoolboy to young secular man at the beginning of his adult life. Spinning without control might be understood as emblematic for what awaited Ray in the years to come, years directed by adventure, chance and opportunism rather than determined control over a selected path.

Despite his early renunciations of his own different-ness and the desire to fit in to what he saw as a cultural norm, Ray became, in the next stage of his life, perfectly comfortable not fitting in; not in a religious sense, but he learned to distrust easy truths, popular favourites, crowd reactions. Instead, he chose to sit more on the edges of society, to be a bit of a contrarian and attempt, without any great success, alternative ways of living.

This was accompanied by a period of existential malaise, of deeply felt uncertainties, except for the desolate certainty of his own aloneness. Would the easy comfort that came from being a part of his earlier community, of unquestioningly accepting his Jewish origins and a continuation of the ritualistic patterns of behaviour that followed, have helped him through this period? Did his rejection of this commitment create the ground for the later malaise? Maybe the cosmic joke would not have seemed quite so tragi-comic? Despite Ray's resistance, his Jewishness was indelibly embedded – like it or not, he was the product of his own history and circumstances. And this emerged more forcefully for him as time passed. He was struck by the familiarity and ease he felt with other Jewish people living in different countries of the world, a kind of tribal identification that came through the consistency of a shared culture and ethnic base, and a view of life that had a distinctive timbre filtered by Yiddish humour.

Ray's world at the age of eighteen was remarkably different from the world of his early childhood, so soon after World War II and the Holocaust. His childhood in the 1950s was set in a religious milieu where Australians were either Protestants or Catholics and they did not comfortably mix. There were very few outliers – and they were treated with some suspicion or even pity. This was a time when mothers were all performing home duties, not in paid work, and when they went to 'town' they dressed up, wearing white gloves and hats.

Like many Australians of this period, Ray's father was an Anglophile and a monarchist, in his case, stemming from time in the Australian Navy and his admiration for what he saw of the English Navy during the war. Ray was unable to share these enthusiasms and he found it bizarre that, at this time, Australian Broadcasting Commission newscasters were obliged to speak in a BBC-like accent, emphasising the outpost condition of Australia.

It was a time when many Australians from the Anglo-Celt vast majority referred to Great Britain as 'home'. Even though they may never have been there, they considered this faraway country as their real home, their time in Australia as some sort of temporary exile. This was not the case for Jewish Australians, including Ray, who had originated from other than a British source. Of these, many regarded the newly formed state of Israel as 'home' and Ray knew quite a number of contemporaries who, as soon as they were able to do so, migrated there and committed their lives to helping build the Jewish state. Ray never felt any such urge and was deeply puzzled later in life when his brother, who had become a pilot, was keen to join the Israeli Air Force.

His brother later explained that, unlike Ray, he was a 'Zionist-at-heart' but the complicated process involved in joining the Air Force had defeated his desire.

This story was written at the other end of the young life we have described, at a time when a finish to that life is comprehensible and very much closer. Ray, of course, understands this must be so, that this time death will be ready for him – but he is bewildered in the knowledge that his life experience, rich and not so rich, will disappear with him. This, then, is a diffident attempt to add aspects of his humble life to that great ocean of experience and learning that fills the bookshelves of libraries and provides witness to the process and struggles of being human.

This has been but one of many, many tales that could have been told from that early photograph, life trajectories through which we stumble or steer, and set our directions for the lives that follow.

It's best to give while your hand is still warm.

Philip Roth, *Everyman*

About Upswell

Upswell Publishing was established in 2021 by Terri-ann White as a not-for-profit press. A perceived gap in the market for distinctive literary works in fiction, poetry and narrative non-fiction was the motivation. In her years as a bookseller, writer and then publisher, Terri-ann has maintained a watch on literary books and the way they insinuate themselves into a cultural space and are then located within our literary and cultural inheritance. She is interested in making books to last: books with the potential to still be noticed, and noted, after decades and thus be ripe to influence new literary histories.